Celebrating 100 Years
UMD
DULUTH

UMD COMES OF AGE

The First One Hundred Years
by Ken Moran and Neil Storch

with the assistance of
Doreen Hansen, Lucy Kragness, Jackie Moran,
Mary Morse, and James Vileta

Copyright © 1996 by The University of Minnesota Duluth

All rights reserved, including the right to reproduce this work in any form whatsoever without permission in writing from the publisher, except for brief passages in connection with a review. For information, write:

The Donning Company/Publishers
184 Business Park Drive, Suite 106
Virginia Beach, Virginia 23462

Steve Mull, General Manager
Nancy Schneiderheinze, Project Director
Mair Downing, Project Research Coordinator
Chris Decker, Graphic Designer
Elizabeth Bobbitt, Executive Editor
Dawn V. Kofroth, Production Manager
Tony Lillis, Director of Marketing

Library of Congress Cataloging in Publication Data:

Moran, Ken.
    UMD comes of age : the first one hundred years / by Ken Moran and Neil Storch.
        p.   cm.
    Includes index.
    ISBN 0-89865-970-1 (hardcover : alk. paper)
    1. University of Minnesota, Duluth-History. 2. Indians of North America-Education (Higher)-Minnesota-Duluth-History.
I. Storch, Neil. II. Title.
LD3318.M67 1996
378.776'771-dc20   96-18263

                        CIP

Printed in the United States of America

CONTENTS

FOREWORD
7

ACKNOWLEDGMENTS
9

CHAPTER ONE
THE FOUNDING OF UMD
A COMMUNITY EFFORT
1895-1938
13

CHAPTER TWO
DSTC TO UMD
THE TRANSITION YEARS
1938-1947
29

CHAPTER THREE
GIBSON AND KING
THE EARLY VISION
1947-1953
45

CHAPTER FOUR
UMD COMES OF AGE
THE DARLAND YEARS
1953-1976
75

UMD REFLECTIONS
132

CHAPTER FIVE
ROBERT HELLER
THE GROWING MATURITY OF UMD
1976-1987
145

CHAPTER SIX
THE IANNI YEARS
A DECADE OF GROWTH
1987-1995
179

CHRONOLOGY
208

UMD REFLECTIONS II
212

INDEX
218

ABOUT THE AUTHORS
224

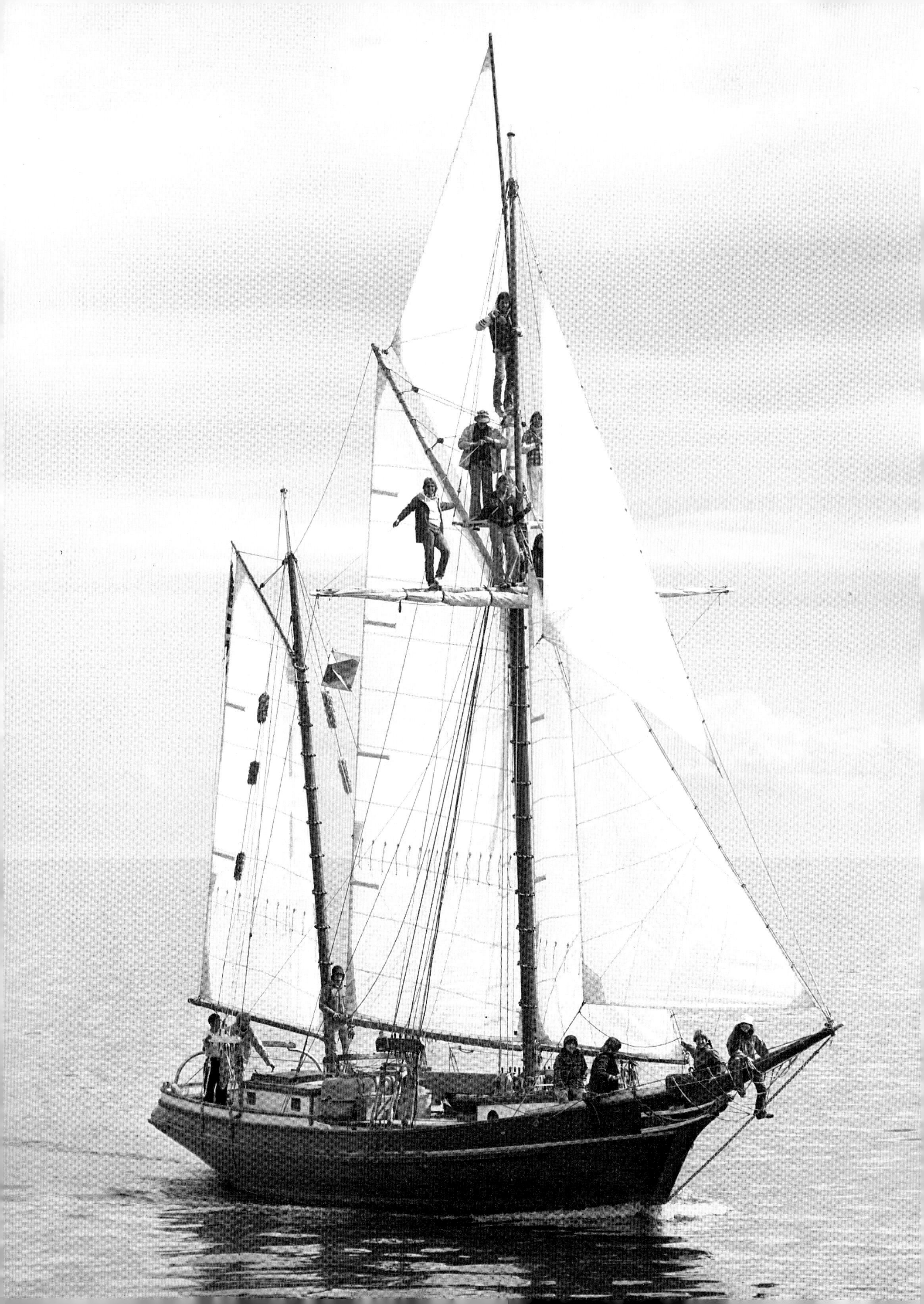

FOREWORD

One hundred years is a significant milestone for any institution, proof that it has been able to adjust to and accommodate change. As this book attests, UMD's willingness to explore new educational territory has been one of its strengths throughout its first century. Many of its greatest successes have also been its greatest risks. As we move into UMD's second century, we must never forget how our ability to take risks created what we have become. Without risktakers, Duluth State Teachers College would not have become the University of Minnesota Duluth. Without risktakers, UMD would not have the School of Medicine or the Natural Resources Research Institute or the Tweed Museum of Art or the Large Lakes Observatory. Without risktakers, UMD would not have gained national recognition for its academic, athletic, and arts achievements, its emphasis upon faculty research and teaching, its undergraduate research opportunities, and its innovative responses to regional educational, economic, and human services needs. The risktakers were UMD's former presidents, provosts, and chancellors. They were faculty and staff members committed to the idea that a university education provides an indispensable foundation for life. They were community members who believed UMD's successes led to an improved quality of life in Duluth and northeastern Minnesota. And above all, they were the students who chose UMD. This book is their story.

As of this writing, I have been UMD's chancellor for almost two hundred days. I have spent many hours with UMD alumni throughout the country. I have learned about their involvement with education, with youth, with government, with business and industry, with medicine, and with other human services. I am proud to know these committed, caring people began their adult lives as UMD students. Our alumni constantly demonstrate their strong loyalty to UMD with their gifts to us and their involvement in our programs. Their contributions reflect a genuine appreciation for the quality education and personalized attention they received here. And as they have so often done before, they have rallied behind our efforts to build the new library we so desperately need for the twenty-first century.

The new paradigm for a university education reflects and responds to the needs of a global society. For UMD that paradigm translates into a dual mission. We must continue to create and support programs which meet the specific needs of our region. But we also must prepare our students for futures which may take them anywhere in the world. And because instilling social values remains a primary goal of a UMD education, we will continue to offer programs that emphasize compassion, justice, and integrity just as much as learning career skills. Your continued support will help us make UMD everything it deserves to be in its second hundred years.

KATHRYN A. MARTIN, Chancellor

ACKNOWLEDGMENTS

This book celebrating the first one hundred years of the University of Minnesota Duluth (UMD) is a "popular" account that provides a pictorial overview and a condensed history of the Duluth Normal School, Duluth State Teachers College, and the University of Minnesota Duluth. It was a labor of love. The project involved hundreds of people who treasure UMD. Thousands of photographs were examined. The photographs presented in this book are only the tip of the proverbial iceberg. We thank the photographers represented here as well as all the other photographers whose skills created the visual history of this institution. They captured the heart and soul of the campus.

The outstanding archival collections organized and managed by James J. Vileta, UMD's archivist, provided a wealth of official correspondence, memoranda, reports, minutes, speeches, newspaper clippings, bulletins, and yearbooks. An annotated bibliography of the sources used in this project can be consulted in the UMD Archives. Vileta's work in the archives over the last two decades made this book possible. In addition to their invaluable work in the UMD Archives, Vileta and Doreen L. Hansen, assistant archivist, have compiled and edited an informative chronology of UMD's history. A brief excerpt from their chronology appears in the appendix of this volume.

We also appreciate the efforts of Patricia Maus of the Northeastern Minnesota Historical Center, located on the UMD campus. She made available valuable collections of the St. Louis County Historical Society. Jackie Moran, an oral historian working with technical assistance from Doreen Hansen, conducted a series of highly informative videotaped interviews that provided much of the material for this book. The oral history project is ongoing. We thank all those present and retired administrators, faculty members, staff, regents, alumni, and friends of UMD who shared their knowledge of the past and their love of UMD with us. It was indeed moving to see how deeply the people interviewed cared about UMD and its students.

Thanks to the members of the celebration committee chaired by Harry Oden for their commitment and hard work. Their efforts made it possible to celebrate UMD's centennial with this volume. Special thanks to Robert Falk, Stephen Hedman, Bruce Rutherford, and Diane Skomars for their ideas and belief that UMD's story needed to be told. We are indebted to Lucy Kragness, UMD's alumni director, for her research and caption writing for the photo essay chapter, "The Ianni Years." The volume also contains two provocative essays by Frank McCray and Beatrice Ojakangas, alumni of UMD. We are proud of their achievements, and we welcome their thoughts about their Alma Mater. We also thank the UMD *Statesman* and *The Duluthian* for permission to reprint the essays by Professor Klaus Jankofsky and former Chancellor Lawrence Ianni.

We appreciate the assistance of Mary Morse, University Relations acting publications director, who served as our UMD editor; Alexis Pogorelskin, Department of History associate professor and chair, who also read the manuscript and provided helpful suggestions; Bob Nygaard, UMD sports information director; Teri Johnson, acting public relations director; and Betsy Bobbitt, our editor at Donning Company Publishers.

Very special appreciation goes to former Chancellor Lawrence A. Ianni, who encouraged the project in its initial phases. Ianni since has returned to the classroom as a professor of English and continues his active interest in the project. We also are deeply indebted to Chancellor Kathryn A. Martin for her encouragement and support and wish her well as she guides UMD into the twenty-first century. We hope this brief glimpse of UMD's history expresses the tenacious "Bulldog" spirit of the campus. We are deeply grateful to all who forged that spirit.

KEN MORAN AND NEIL STORCH

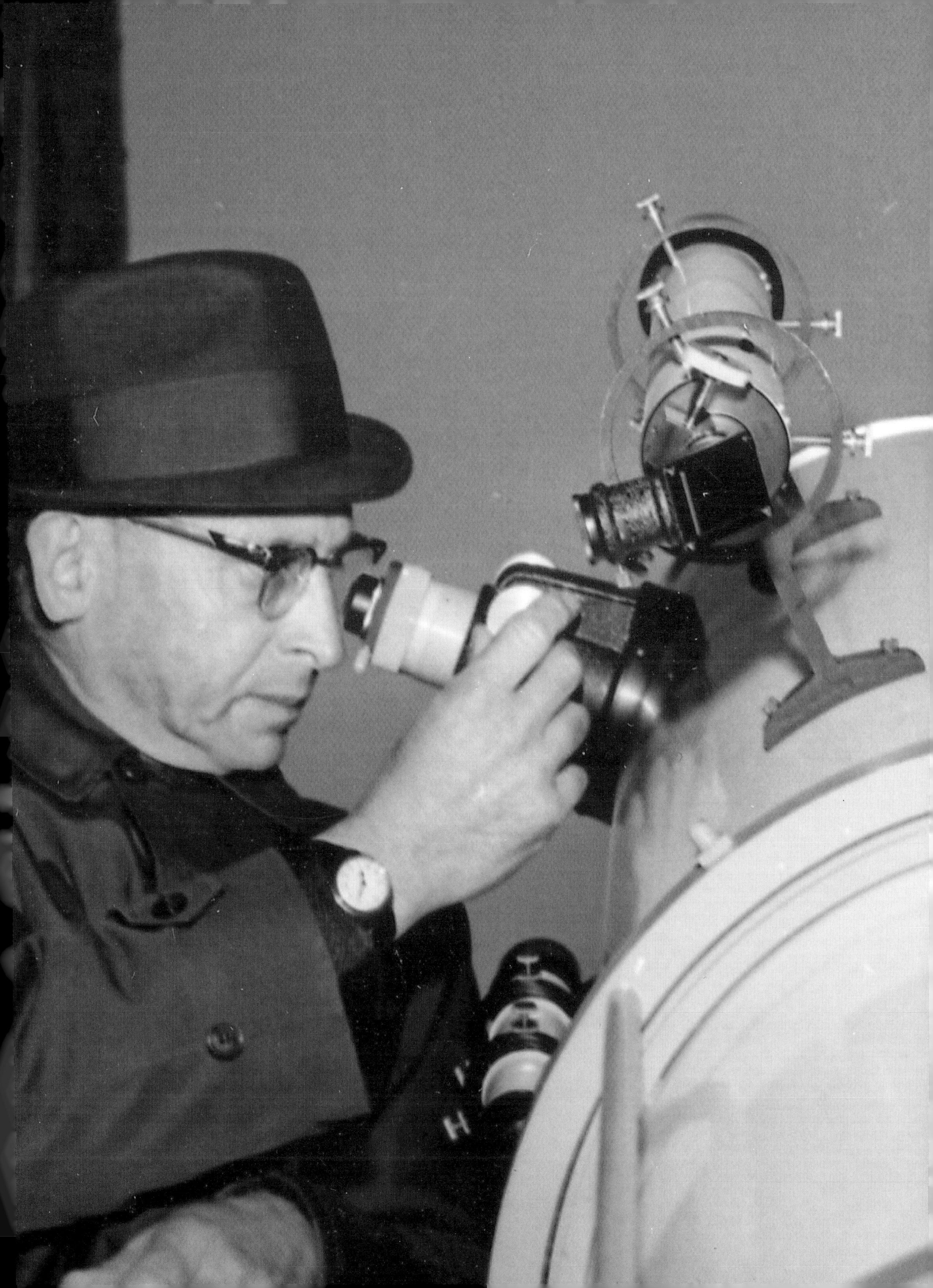

The annual May Fete was celebrated on the grounds of the Duluth Normal School to welcome the coming of spring. The last May Fete was held at Duluth State Teachers College (DSTC) in 1940.

THE FOUNDING OF UMD: A COMMUNITY EFFORT

1895–1938

CHAPTER ONE

The University of Minnesota Duluth did not just happen—it is the product of dreams, hopes, and determination. To understand its origin and growth, we must journey back in time to April 2, 1895, when the Minnesota State Legislature authorized a normal school in Duluth to train elementary school teachers. Agitation for the school had begun in the 1880s, but was not successful in the state legislature until 1895, when political horse trading finally carried the day. As we celebrate the University of Minnesota Duluth's (hereafter UMD) centennial, we must remember that public higher education in Duluth has always depended on community support. Northern Minnesota civic leaders, legislators, and educators fought to create and develop the Duluth Normal School, Duluth State Teachers College (hereafter DSTC), and UMD.

The opening of the Duluth Normal School, UMD's earliest predecessor, was delayed by a lack of money and a severe fire that destroyed the school's only building before it was completed. The building was reconstructed. When the first students registered in the fall of 1902, they found a one-building campus with a spectacular view of Lake Superior. There were no paved streets nearby. Occasionally a stray cow wandered on campus to graze on the new lawn. Staffed with a faculty of ten, including President Eugene W. Bohannon, the Normal School had an enrollment of fewer than one hundred students.

DR. E. W. BOHANNON SELECTED

MANKATO MAN IS MADE PRESIDENT OF DULUTH NORMAL.

Chosen Out of Twenty Candidates---Normal Board Puts Itself Under the Board of Control.

Dr. E. W. Bohannon, for three years superintendent of the training department of the Mankato Normal, was on Saturday selected for the position of president of the Duluth Normal, by the State Normal Board, in session at St. Paul. There were twenty candidates for the place.

Dr. Bohannon is 35 years of age. He graduated from the Indiana State Normal School in the class of 1887. He received the A. B. degree from the University of Indiana in 1890, and the A. M. degree in 1892. He spent three years, 1895-1898, at the Clark University at Worcester, Mass., in study for the doctor of philosophy.

On April 22, 1901, the *Mankato Daily* announced the appointment of Dr. E. W. Bohannon as the first president of the Duluth Normal School.

E. W. Bohannon took office on September 2, 1901. Bohannon was hired at a salary of $2,500 per year.

Most of the women attending Duluth Normal were eighth-grade graduates pursuing a five-year high school course with emphasis on Latin or English and professional training in education. Graduates earned teaching diplomas and were certified to teach in Minnesota's elementary schools. High school graduates could enroll in a two-year program and be certified to teach. In response to higher standards mandated by the state, Duluth Normal raised its admission standards in 1916 by requiring a high school diploma.

Much of the history of Duluth Normal School and DSTC centers on Bohannon, the institution's first president, who assumed office in 1901 and remained until 1938. Though not tall, the distinguished looking president stood so erect that he seemed to tower over his surroundings. A man of integrity and ideals, Bohannon once declared that if people who "serve as teachers have not the character to remain free and uncontrolled in their thinking and acting, they have no right to be teaching." He urged teachers to focus on their students and subject disciplines without becoming method-ridden.

NORMAL FOR DULUTH

State Normal Board Authorizes Opening of Building Sept. 2

PROSPECTS ARE GOOD

President Bohannon Says There Will Be an Attendance of at Least 100 at the First Term.

After two years of agitation and disappointment, Duluth's new normal school is to open at last. The state normal board yesterday authorized the opening of the school on Tuesday, September 2, the board of control having pledged itself to have the building ready by that time.

The June 15, 1902, edition of the *St. Paul Pioneer Press* announced the September opening of the Duluth Normal School.

Class '03

The first graduates of the Duluth Normal School were Amanda Elefson, Aonas Rebecca Holt, Bessie Emily Bowmann, Elizabeth Merritt, Willena Marie Marshall, Helen Emily Bowyer, and Esther Levy.

Margaret Culkin Banning, a noted Duluth author whose home overlooked the original campus on East Fifth Street, remembered Duluth Normal's first president as a man who "truly believed that teaching was the most distinguished profession in the world." She recalls that Bohannon set the school's high cultural tone by gathering a faculty who believed that the women who came there to prepare for careers in elementary education "should not only be grounded in teaching skills but also become aware of cultural traditions and forces."

Banning had vivid memories of several faculty members, especially those in the English department: Marjorie Strong, a lover of poetry; Katherine Post, an astute critic of literature; and Charles Saltus, a Chaucer scholar. Among the outstanding faculty members noted by Banning were the teachers at the laboratory or training school where the aspiring teachers of DSTC and UMD did their practice teaching. Four teachers stood out for Banning: Olive Horne, Virginia Willcuts, Helen Urquhart, and her own sister Mabel Culkin. These women individualized the work done with each child and provided a first-rate education. It was a "good break" for parents such as Banning to be able to enroll their children in this fine school. It was a sad day for many when the old "lab" school finally closed its doors in June 1966.

In the formative years, while the foundations for higher education in Duluth were being laid, President Bohannon garnered community support. J. L. Washburn stands out. This prominent city attorney represented Duluth on the Normal School Board, donated money, worked closely with Bohannon, and participated in the day-to-day life of the school. He was frequently on campus visiting classes and giving talks on historical figures and themes. Given Washburn's commitment to education and his lifelong interest in history, it was most appropriate that his friends honored his memory with a fund that granted awards to outstanding students of history. These awards still are granted annually by the UMD Department of History.

*The Faculty and Graduating Class
of the
State Normal School
at Duluth, Minnesota
request the honor of your presence at the
First Annual Commencement Exercises
May thirty-first - June third
nineteen hundred and three
Normal Hall*

This photo of the campus, circa 1906, shows Old Main, Washburn Hall (center), and the Bohannon residence (far right). Washburn Hall, built with a $6,000 gift from J. L. Washburn, a Duluth attorney, was the first campus dormitory. Old Main, the only building on campus when the Minnesota State Legislature authorized the opening of Duluth Normal School in 1901, continued as a classroom site until the 1980s. Old Main was destroyed by fire on February 23, 1993.

The First Annual Commencement Exercises were held in Normal Hall (Old Main) from May 31 through June 3, 1903.

Students gathered for the Duluth Normal School's first "Assembly Hall" in Old Main.

The close friendship and working relationship between Bohannon and Washburn heavily influenced the development of the Normal School. Fortunately, the administrative heads of DSTC and UMD were able to continue to form effective partnerships with community leaders and benefactors. Washburn's friend Stephen Kirby was later instrumental in establishing a student center at UMD. The long-standing partnership and friendship of Provost Raymond Darland and University of Minnesota Regent Richard L. Griggs, a dynamic business and civic leader, also recalled the earlier Bohannon/Washburn relationship.

No discussion of the school's founding figures would be complete without noting the presence of Max Weber, a Russian-born artist who came to Duluth in 1903. Weber taught at Duluth Normal for two years and painted the set for the school's drama production of *Antigone*. In 1905 he left for Europe where he came to know Henri Rousseau, Matisse, and Picasso. Returning to America in 1908, Weber established his reputation as the foremost synthesizer of the latest trends in European art.

There was a closeness—a special bond—among the women studying at Duluth Normal. The women shared the common career goal of training as teachers, one of the few job opportunities then open to women. Women at the school often built friendships that lasted a lifetime as they shared the precious opportunity for higher education that teacher training offered them.

The annual May Fete was an important event for the women on campus. This joyous celebration heralded the arrival of spring with music and dance. Popular with students both at Duluth Normal and DSTC, it also delighted townspeople who sought coveted tickets and eagerly flocked to the celebration. The festival, with its frilly costumes, May Queen, and traditional dance around the Maypole, no longer suited the ambiance of the school once men enrolled in significant numbers. The last such ceremony was held at DSTC in 1940.

The women of Duluth Normal were keenly interested in the issue of women's suffrage. Women had been demanding the right to vote in Minnesota since the founding of the state in 1858. The graduating class of 1906 must have listened with mixed emotions to the commencement address of University of Minnesota Professor S. F. Jones as he stressed the role of teachers in fostering well-informed voters. The irony of women, who could not vote themselves, teaching good citizenship to their male students was certainly not lost on the graduates. The women at Duluth Normal continued to debate the issue and some worked to change the law. Their efforts were rewarded in 1919, when Minnesota women won the right to vote for president, a year ahead of the constitutional amendment which granted women's suffrage.

DULUTH STATE TEACHERS COLLEGE

In April 1921 the Minnesota Legislature followed national trends and reorganized its normal schools into teachers colleges. In addition to the traditional two-year program leading to a teaching diploma, the State Teachers College Board was now authorized to establish a four-year program leading to a college degree. The first bachelor degrees were awarded at DSTC in 1927.

By 1927 DSTC had more than twenty faculty members and eight hundred students. The campus sprawled across nine acres with four buildings—an expanded Old Main, two dormitories, and an elementary school for practice teaching. Despite its impressive growth, the school remained largely a college for women in its first decade. This was soon to change.

The students of DSTC did their first practice teaching in the Laboratory School located at 2205 East Fifth Street, dedicated in 1927. The building later became the first School of Medicine, then the first home of the Natural Resources Research Institute, and now is the Research Laboratory Building.

Torrance Hall, the second women's dormitory to be built on campus, was named after Judge Eli Torrance, president of the State Normal Board. The dormitory opened in 1910. Above, early residents of Torrance Hall posed for a group portrait.

Students used the resources of the first campus library to pursue their studies. Today, UMD's library holdings consist of more than 400,000 volumes, 2,000-plus periodical subscriptions, 10,000-plus films, recordings, and other non-print items, and 262,000 government documents.

Mabel Culkin, left, sister of Duluth novelist Margaret Culkin Banning, was one of the outstanding educators who taught and supervised student teachers in the Laboratory School setting. Many Duluthians sent their children to UMD's Laboratory School, which closed in June 1966.

The bulldog became DSTC's official team mascot in 1933.

Max Weber, a Russian-born artist, came to Duluth Normal School in 1903. He created the backdrops for the student production of *Antigone*, staged at Duluth Normal School on June 6, 1904. Weber was photographed in 1951, when he returned to UMD to teach a summer art class.

Duluth Normal School encouraged its women students to learn woodworking and other shop skills in its manual arts classes.

Left: Home economics was considered a vital part of Duluth Normal School's curriculum in 1912.

Duluth Normal School students enjoyed spring fun on campus.

The Normal School Auditorium was added to Old Main in 1915.

Duluth Normal School students portrayed Robin Hood and his band.

The dramatic increase in the number of men was the result of a revision in the teacher certification law that allowed teachers colleges to prepare students for positions in high schools as well as elementary schools. In addition, many men searching for work during the Great Depression found teaching an attractive career opportunity. The number of men enrolled jumped from less than ten in 1929 to more than two hundred in 1931. Though men remained a distinct minority, about 20 percent from 1931 to 1937, their presence profoundly affected campus life. For example, within a few years men tended to dominate class offices such as president and vice president while women were relegated to the post of class secretary.

School spirit rose as the men introduced intercollegiate competition in basketball, football, and track. Homecoming events and a downtown parade of cars and trucks decorated

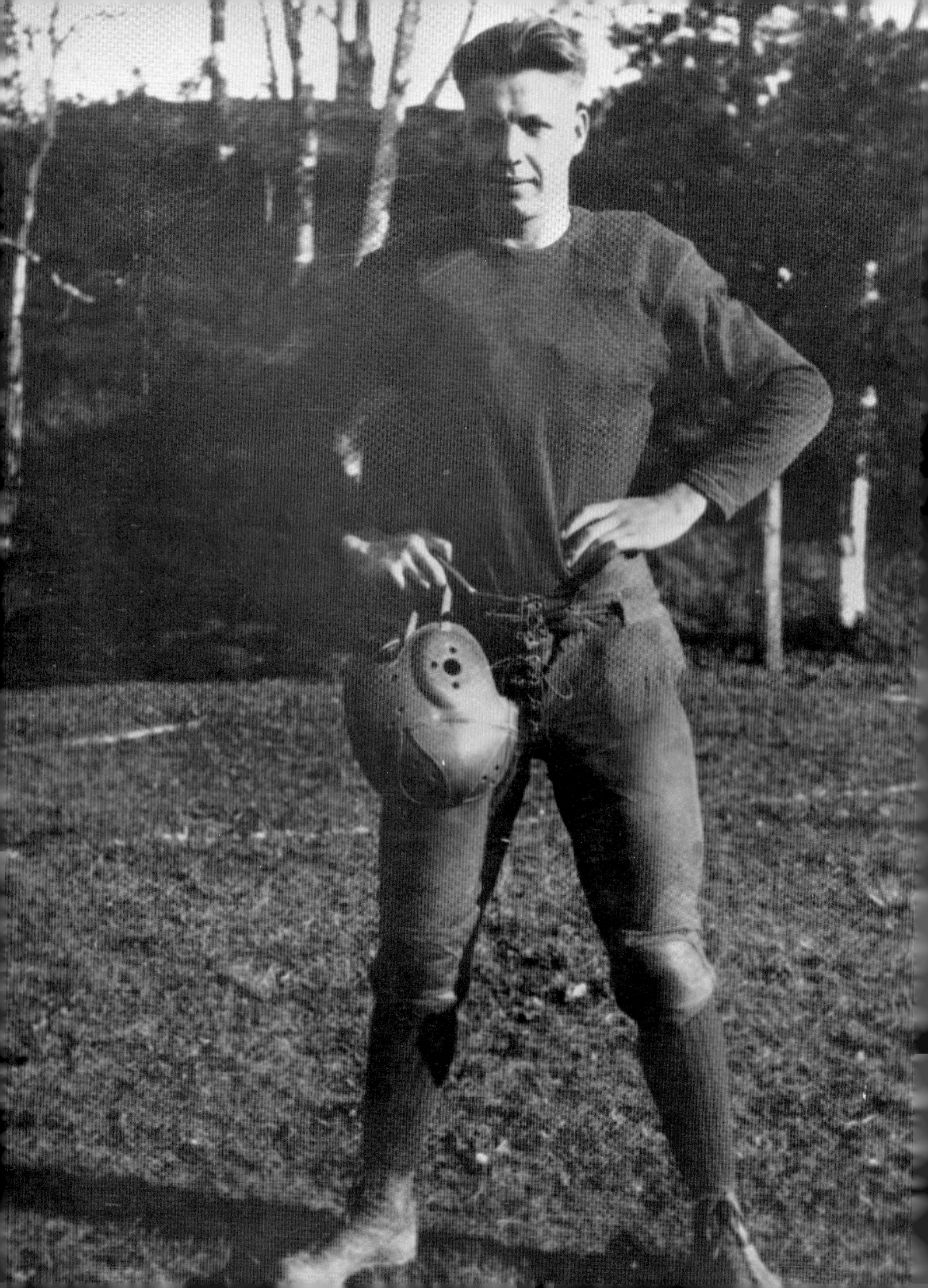

in green and gold—the original school colors—added to the excitement. The school now needed a symbol or mascot. The traditional designation of "peds" for pedagogues or teachers no longer sufficed. What team would rally to cries of "go peds!"? In the spring of 1933 the athletes themselves picked the bulldog as the school's mascot, and the image has endured. Unwittingly, the athletes had stumbled on a most apt symbol for DSTC's successor, UMD, which owes its existence to the dogged determination of those committed to a university campus in Duluth.

Lloyd W. "Pete" Peterson, physical education, became DSTC's first football coach in 1931. He served as head coach for twenty-four years.

Left: The DSTC football team played its first game against Northland College in Ashland, Wisconsin, on September 30, 1930. Northland won 10-0. Walter Thygeson, one of the team members, posed for this photograph in 1932.

A banner and the 1941 DSTC Homecoming court announced the Saturday Homecoming game to downtown Duluth. Seated in the back, from left to right were Betty Pearson, Homecoming Queen Eleanor Wigg, Jane Latham, and Virginia Giliuson. Seated in the front passenger seat was Lloyd Luukkonen.

DSTC TO UMD: THE TRANSITION YEARS

1938–1947

CHAPTER TWO

The retirement of President Bohannon in the winter of 1938 marked the end of an era. His leadership was most evident in the growth of the faculty from ten, when the school opened in 1902, to more than forty—including ten Ph.D.s—when his retirement was announced in 1937. Though he left an impressive legacy, his retirement in fact opened the door for needed change. Bohannon had believed that DSTC should focus exclusively on teacher training rather than expand into a comprehensive college that granted liberal arts degrees.

His successor, Herbert Sorenson, an associate professor of education at the University of Minnesota, was inaugurated as president in 1938. After studying the educational needs of the region, he decided that DSTC must offer liberal arts as well as teaching degrees. His ultimate goal was to transform the college into a branch of the University of Minnesota. Sorenson's effort to make DSTC part of the University strained relations with the State Teachers Board because the board did not want to lose a campus.

Sorenson began by insisting on high professional standards. Some instructors, disgruntled by the president's desire to get rid of "weak" faculty and his "neglect" of certain departments, took

DSTC President Herbert Sorenson, left, met with Dr. Frank J. Hirschbock. Hirschbock, a Duluth physician, was appointed to the Minnesota State Teachers College Board on September 23, 1941. In October 1941 he was appointed resident director of DSTC, succeeding Viena Johnson.

offense at his "direct" and at times "explosive" remarks. His manner stood in sharp contrast to the measured, gentlemanly ways of Bohannon.

In March 1946, the State Teachers College Board ordered that charges against Sorenson be drawn up. The faculty divided into warring camps. Students, motivated by Sorenson's hiring of outstanding faculty and the growing reputation of their college, circulated a pro-Sorenson petition and ultimately shut down the campus with a strike. Many prominent citizens also rallied to Sorenson's defense. But in the end the beleaguered president, his voice breaking, explained to the students that he had to resign. Students wept openly.

The imbroglio was over. Under Acting President Ezra H. Pieper, who held the office while a search for a new president was being conducted, the college quieted down. The conflict with Sorenson was over, but not the campaign to transform DSTC. Those who favored an expanded mission for DSTC adopted Sorenson's arguments.

Sorenson's successor, Raymond C. Gibson, joined the campaign spearheaded by Minnesota State Representative A. B. Anderson of Duluth to transform DSTC into a comprehensive college which would grant liberal arts degrees. A Duluth delegation attended a meeting of the State Teachers College Board in August 1946, only five months after the board had brought charges against Sorenson. The group argued that the curriculum at DSTC had to be expanded to meet the needs of World War II veterans, not all of whom could be expected to train as teachers. Their arguments swayed the board, and it agreed to authorize liberal arts programs at all the teachers colleges. Even this triumph, heralded in banner headlines, did not satisfy Duluth leaders. The campaign for a University of Minnesota campus continued.

During World War II many male and female DSTC students left for military service. By 1945, 281 male students were in the service. Thirteen were killed in action.

University Of Minnesota, Duluth Branch

Why, after opposing branch campuses for so many years, did the University of Minnesota finally agree to a Duluth branch in 1947? The reversal must be seen in the context of the quarter-century campaign led by public-spirited Duluthians who fought

Professor Emeritus Gerhard E. von Glahn first came to DSTC as a professor of political science in 1941. He left campus in 1943 to serve in the military and returned in 1946. He served as head of the Department of Political Science from 1947 to 1979, when he retired. Nationally, he is known as the author of the definitive study on the occupation of enemy territories, *Law Among Nations*, a widely used textbook in colleges and universities.

In l942, von Glahn and his fiancee Dorothy Grant, who was then head of the Department of Home Economics at DSTC, were married at Tweed Hall, the former Joseph Cotton mansion on Twenty-third Avenue East and First Street donated to UMD in 1941 by Alice and George Tweed. Von Glahn and Grant thought it would be appropriate to inaugurate the building with their wedding ceremony. "Tweed was magnificent—it had sterling silver fixtures in the bathrooms and a ballroom on the top floor," he recalled.

Von Glahn said that his greatest contribution to UMD was "the intellectual development of students—I think I showed them areas that they normally would not have known about."

In 1995 Jim Corson, retired managing editor of West Publishing and a student at UMD in the late 1940s, gave the original gift for the Gerhard E. von Glahn Scholarship. Corson said he was inspired by von Glahn's example as a scholar and a teacher.

In May of 1943 Lois Pearling and Mike Karnis played central roles in the DSTC production of *Victoria Regina*.

for a connection with the University. The dream of a University branch inspired civic leaders to form committees that worked actively to convince University officials and legislators that northern Minnesota taxpayers were not getting a fair return on their educational tax dollar. A branch campus in northern Minnesota would save taxpaying parents thousands of dollars and allow their sons and daughters to earn college degrees. Many students, it was argued, simply could not afford the travel and living expenses of pursuing degrees at the University of Minnesota located in the Twin Cities. Among the outstanding leaders of this vigorous campaign was Proctor Superintendent of Schools A. I. Jedlicka, who chaired two committees. Other community leaders included Mrs. A. A. Mendenhall, A. H. Ahlen, Dr. W. R. Bagley, Arthur M. Clure, Frank Crassweller, Harold A. Lyon, Edward A. Martini, Mrs. W. C. Smith, Mrs. Felix Seligman, Gerald A. Myles, and Julius F. Wolff, Sr. Wolff wrote two widely-distributed pamphlets advocating a Duluth branch. Undaunted by opposition from University of Minnesota officials, Duluth-area citizens, through their unwavering dedication and hard work, formulated cogent arguments which eventually created UMD.

The campaign for a Duluth branch was put in abeyance from 1941 to 1945 because of World War II. In early December 1941, a young political science professor, Gerhard E. von Glahn, was preparing a radio show on "Japan and the United States" for the DSTC radio program to be broadcast on December 8! After the Japanese attack on Pearl Harbor on December 7, von Glahn hastily revised his script.

These DSTC faculty members steered their students toward challenging and rewarding careers in teaching.

Mary I. Elwell, mathematics

Frank Kovach, industrial education and Bulldog coach

Maude L. Lindquist, history and sociology

R. Dale Miller, music

While men remained a minority—about 20 percent during the Great Depression—among DSTC students, their presence greatly affected campus social life. Above, students danced to the sounds of the Lloyd Hawley Band.

Community leaders vigorously renewed the campaign for a University branch at the end of the war, seizing the opportunities afforded by the rapid expansion of higher education after World War II. Veterans utilizing the Servicemen's Readjustment Act, better known as the G.I. Bill, flooded the University of Minnesota's Minneapolis campus. Unable to meet student demand, University officials were now confronted with an emotional question with profound political implications: How could veterans, who had risked their lives for their country, be denied an opportunity to attend the University of Minnesota?

Vice President Malcolm M. Willey, realizing that the expansion of higher education outside the Twin Cities could not

Olga Lakela, a science and mathematics professor and botanist, wrote seventy-five publications about Minnesota plants and birds. Her herbarium included more than ten thousand plants. Lakela taught and researched at DSTC and UMD for more than fifty years (1935 to 1978).

be stopped, spelled out the stark realities for President James L. Morrill. Willey warned that the University of Minnesota would either have to make the teachers colleges branches or face the unsettling prospect that they would become the University's competitors. The University's newfound willingness to discuss the possibility of a branch campus in Duluth also was engendered by its need for political support. Given the need for rapid expansion to accommodate the returning veterans, University officials were not in a position to offend northern legislators such as State Representative A. B. Anderson.

Duluth attorney James G. Nye, sensing that the University was abandoning its longstanding opposition to branch campuses, searched the Territorial Act of February 25, 1851, to determine how the DSTC could legally become part of the University of Minnesota. He realized that "the State Teachers College Board was, in legal effect, a board of trustees, and it

Jim McIntyre led the DSTC Bulldogs to victory in the fall of 1941.

The Fall Freshman Dance was the 1940s version of a "freshman mixer."

Alice and George Tweed purchased the Joseph Cotton mansion on Twenty-third Avenue East and First Street and then gave it to DSTC in 1941. The mansion housed the art department until 1958, when the department moved to the new Humanities building.

Early DSTC cheerleaders were both men and women. The 1941–42 cheerleading team included Jane Latham, Alyce Taylor, John Grandchamp, Betty Lehman, and Sue Green.

Mary Ryan, left, and Eleanor Wigg studied in their room in Torrance Hall.

might qualify, under the wording of the act, to apply to the Regents to receive the DSTC 'into connection with the University.'" Nye reasoned that if the Minnesota State Legislature passed an enabling act sanctioning the transfer, and the University of Minnesota accepted the campus, there would be no legal obstacle.

To lobby for approval, Nye called together a group consisting of those with a longstanding commitment to converting DSTC into a branch campus of the University of Minnesota. Later the following blue-ribbon subcommittee, with Nye as chair, was established from this group; its members included Margaret Culkin Banning, Fred W. Buck, Arthur M. Clure, and Charles F. Liscomb. With the active support of University of Minnesota Regent Richard L. Griggs, the subcommittee was able to meet with University President Morrill and his vice presidents. The historic meeting, which took place on December 10, 1946, was congenial, and Dr. Morrill agreed to present the Duluth proposal to the Board of Regents. The Regents, after several meetings and long discussion, finally

DSTC students and their dates enjoyed the 1941 Spring Prom.

approved a cautious resolution supporting a University campus in Duluth.

DSTC President Raymond C. Gibson proved helpful in the campaign to create UMD. Nye reported that, because of Gibson's official position, "it was impossible for him to be as openly active as he desired to be, but from the very beginning he was enthusiastic about the idea, although there was no assurance whatsoever that he would be continued in office under the new regime. He saw what the project would mean to Duluth and northern Minnesota, and, without consideration of his personal status, he did everything that he legitimately could do to bring about the change."

The struggle now shifted to the Minnesota State Legislature where Representative Anderson led an uphill battle. In addition to Anderson and other Duluth-area legislators, Nye credited the victory to the large number of Duluthians who enthusiastically lobbied for a Duluth branch. To help ensure passage of Anderson's bill, Duluthians promised University officials and legislators that they would buy a site for a new campus. This offer cleared the way for serious consideration of a University branch in Duluth. The 160-acre Nortondale Tract, the site of

DSTC students registered for classes in the fall of 1941.

DSTC students took a study break in their dorm room.

Right: The Women's Athletic Association hosted the annual "College Playdays." The theme in February 1942 was "Reaching for the Stars."

Freshman Helen Rantala was crowned Homecoming queen during special ceremonies on the football field in 1942. The Bulldogs defeated Winona.

today's campus, was purchased by Regent Griggs and other prominent Duluthians. This is but another example of the close relationship between UMD and the community. The purchase was an important step in fulfilling the vision of Sorenson and Gibson, who examined the site and dreamed of a university overlooking Lake Superior.

The generous offer to buy a campus site notwithstanding, Anderson faced a difficult and prolonged struggle in the 1947 legislative session. Vice Provost Emeritus Robert W. Bridges, in his 1989 volume *Campus Buildings and the People for Whom They Are Named*, cites a telling description of Anderson's legislative battle by Minnesota State Legislator Warren S. Moore at the dedication of A. B. Anderson Hall in September 1973. According to Moore, Anderson fought and pleaded for passage of the bill authorizing the transfer of the Duluth campus to the Regents of the University of Minnesota. The valiant legislator "doggedly fought off intense opposition until the closing minutes of the 1947 session."

Moore added: "It so happened that the highway committee of the Senate, of which Clarence Dahl of Duluth was chairman, had adopted a policy of 'No extension of state highways under the Babcock Amendment.' A number of House members wanted an extension of the state highways in their districts. Believing that Mr. Anderson could persuade his senator to lift the road block, they served notice on A. B.: 'Lift the road block or we will kill your college bill in this House, this session.' " Confronted with this challenge, Anderson argued "first with his colleagues

In the final minutes of the 1947 Minnesota legislative session, the House colleagues of A. B. Anderson unanimously voted to support his proposal to make DSTC a branch of the University of Minnesota. In recognition of Anderson's efforts on UMD's behalf, the Classroom-Office Building, constructed between 1968 and 1970, was renamed A. B. Anderson Hall at dedication ceremonies.

Winter garb may have looked different, circa 1944, but the skates and the snow remain enduring symbols of winter in Duluth.

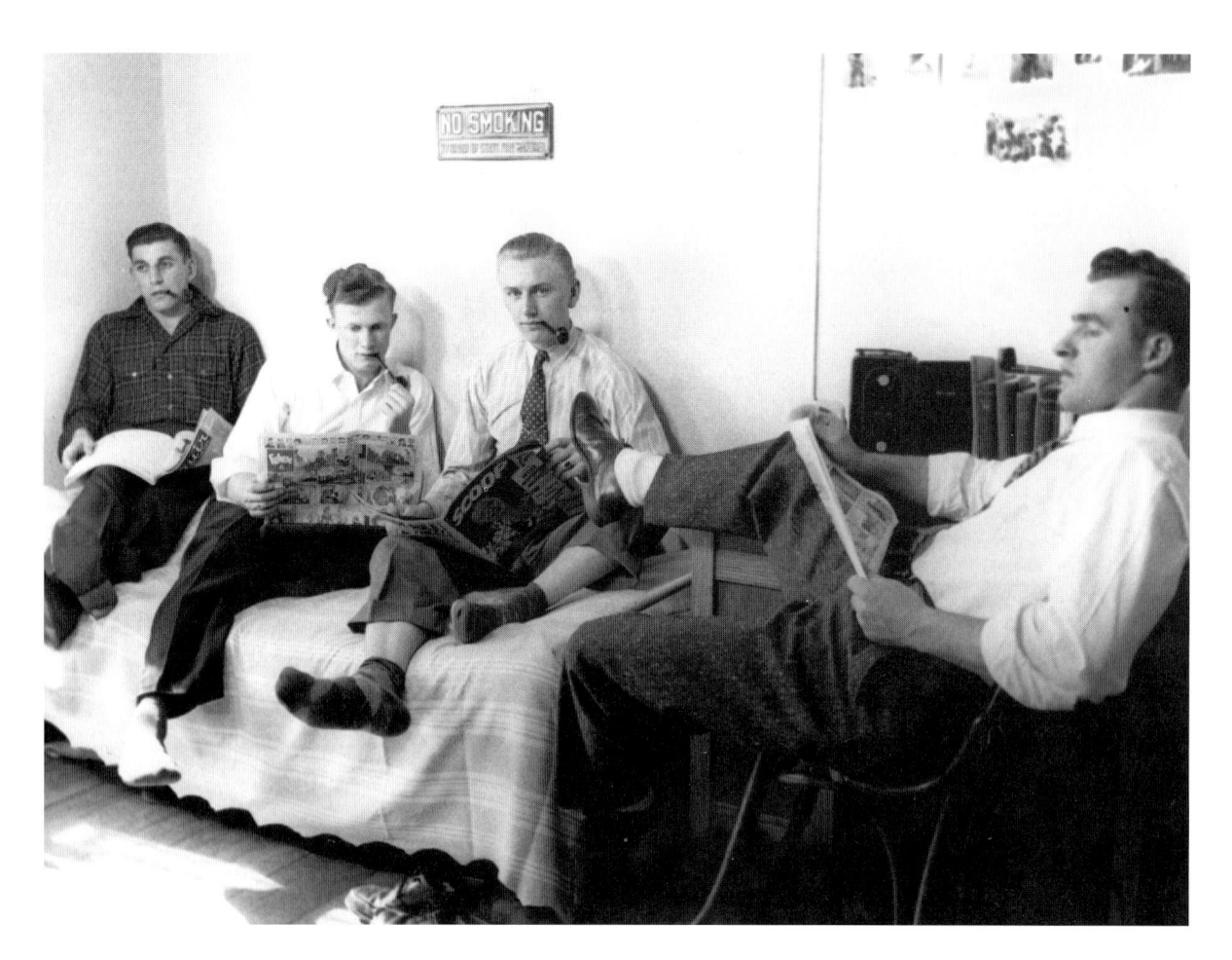

In 1942 several male students relaxed in Washburn Hall. Men moved into the once all-female dormitory in 1936.

in the House, then with Senator Dahl, all to no avail." The impasse continued until the final minutes of the 1947 session when "Roy Dunn, chairman of the rules committee, rose, and facing the House, said 'Mr. Speaker, I move that A. B. Anderson's college bill be given its second and third readings and placed on final passage. Our good friend here has literally been wearing his heart out over this proposed legislation. It's a good bill, and a most worthy project. I am asking every member of this House, every one of you, to support our good friend and colleague A. B. Anderson here and now.' "

Moore reported that the motion carried unanimously. Anderson, amazed and relieved, "succumbed to emotion." As soon as the measure passed, a dozen or more legislators leaped from their seats to congratulate the beaming Anderson. Reflecting on the victory, Moore said, "It was A.B.'s character, fully recognized by every House member, and the wholehearted respect by every one in the chamber, that carried the bill through those closing minutes that day." Anderson's bill was rushed to the Senate, where it passed. Governor Luther W. Youngdahl signed the bill, and on July 1, 1947, the University of Minnesota, Duluth Branch was born. The dream had become a reality.

Louis Baleziak, chemistry professor, demonstrated a laboratory experiment to a DSTC student in the early 1940s.

On July 1, 1947, Minnesota Governor Luther Youngdahl signed the bill which made Duluth State Teachers College the University of Minnesota, Duluth Branch.

Provost Raymond Gibson awarded a diploma to Betty Thomason at a 1947 commencement ceremony. Students Richard Carlson and Robert Falk watched. Falk later became a professor of psychology at UMD.

GIBSON AND KING: THE EARLY VISION

1947–1953

CHAPTER THREE

Raymond Gibson was just thirty-six years old when he assumed the presidency of Duluth State Teachers College on July 1, 1946. He had financed most of his own education, earning bachelor's and master's degrees at Western Kentucky State Teachers College where he studied social studies, English, mathematics, and school administration. In 1944 he received his Ph.D. degree in school administration from the University of Wisconsin-Madison. The range of his teaching and administrative experience extended from small rural schools to city schools, encompassing both grade schools and high schools. When named president of DSTC, he was serving as director of the teacher training and placement department at Stevens Point Teachers College in Wisconsin.

The energetic and idealistic Gibson was expansive in his ideas and vision. He once summed up his profound belief in education as follows: "Education is the most revolutionary thing that can happen to a young person. It is the ultimate step in the achievement of one's freedom."

Given his commitment to education and the post-war expansion of DSTC, it is not surprising that Gibson placed high priority on increasing the quality and size of the faculty. He went

Right: UMD Provost John King, right, explained the model plan of "UMD-1970" to former Minnesota Governor Harold E. Stassen in 1952. The plan featured cottage-like dorms built against a slope for protection against the cold and inside corridors which would make it unnecessary for anyone to venture outside when they went between buildings. Today's UMD students have greatly benefited from his vision.

Left and Above: Wearing UMD beanies was a freshman orientation rite in the early 1950s. Beanies cost just one dollar.

to Duluth convinced that the most important contribution that a president can make to a college or university is to recruit the best possible professors and encourage them to excel. A president should then channel faculty energies, talents, and ambitions to achieve institutional goals. Fortunately, he found that the college already had some outstanding faculty members, excellent teachers capable of providing academic leadership.

In his 1993 autobiography, *From the Hills of Kentucky*, Gibson described some of the outstanding faculty at DSTC. Ezra H. Pieper, the former acting president, was a historian with a Ph.D. from the University of Illinois and he had been teaching at DSTC since 1930. Pieper became a close friend and advisor and proved a strong leader for the Department of Social Studies. Other outstanding professors in social studies included Gerhard E. von Glahn, a political scientist, and Maude L. Lindquist, a historian.

Von Glahn, the same professor who had prepared a radio program on the U.S.-Japan relationship shortly before Japan's attack on Pearl Harbor, returned to DSTC after military service during the war. He developed a strong Department of Political Science and produced authoritative works on international law, specializing in the administration of enemy-occupied territory.

Maude Lindquist, who began her career at DSTC in 1936, was educated at Lawrence College and Columbia University. She later earned her Ph.D. at the University of Minnesota. She applied her knowledge of Minnesota history in her classes and in writing textbooks that were used throughout the state.

Former Homecoming Queen Rose Hable crowned Virginia Christie in 1952 while Dick Wallin watched. Today, Virginia teaches at UMD in the Department of Health, Physical Education, and Recreation. She is married to Bob Murray, former captain of the UMD football team in 1951 and former assistant coach in 1952.

The 1952 Homecoming week activities ended with the annual dance held after the big game. Sweaters for women and suits for men seemed to be in vogue.

Charles N. Saltus, chair of the Department of Languages and Literature, had come to DSTC in 1932 with a Ph.D. from the University of Wisconsin. This outstanding professor, who taught courses on Chaucer, Milton, and Shakespeare, was an extremely popular teacher; his class size was almost always determined by the number of seats in the classroom. Gibson remembered Jackson K. Ehlert, chair of the Department of Fine Arts, as "an aggressive and dynamic leader in building a very strong program." R. Dale Miller, whom Gibson praised as an outstanding musician, had earned an M.A., M.F.A., and Ph.D. from the University of Iowa before joining the music faculty in 1942.

Olga Lakela, chair of the Department of Science and Mathematics, was a distinguished botanist. Gibson remembered that "when asked what budget she needed for laboratory experiments, her reply was that she collected her flora from the woods, fields, and streams of Minnesota." Lakela, who earned her Ph.D. at the University of Minnesota, was a well-known expert on Minnesota plants. Gibson proudly recalled that her herbarium included some ten thousand specimens. This valuable collection is housed today in the Olga Lakela

UMD cheerleaders packed a car for the 1952 Homecoming parade.

49

A former hay meadow constituted the Nortondale Tract purchased by Regent Richard L. Griggs and other prominent Duluthians in the late 1940s. The Science Building, constructed in 1949, was the only building on the new campus until 1953.

An aerial view, circa 1953, showed both the lower and upper campuses.

Herbarium in the College of Science and Engineering. Theron O. Odlaug, a zoologist, who had come to DSTC in 1945 with a Ph.D. from New York University, rounded out a promising program in biology.

Gibson recalled other talented faculty members in the sciences. John C. Cothran, a Cornell University Ph.D., was a professor of chemistry. He cared about his students and simply did not give up until they had mastered the subject. Mary I. Elwell, who had joined the faculty of Duluth Normal School in 1918 with a B.A. from Carleton College and an A.M. from the University of Minnesota, taught mathematics and contributed to campus life, especially the annual May Fete. Another widely respected member of the faculty was Elizabeth Graybeal, chair of the Department of Health and Physical Education. Graybeal, a Ph.D. graduate of the University of Minnesota, had served at DSTC since 1933.

Knowing that enrollment would be more than nine hundred students by the fall of 1946, a 200 percent increase over the previous year, Gibson realized that the faculty would have to be increased by nearly 50 percent. That meant that he would have to recruit eighteen faculty members during his first sixty days as president. Gibson aggressively sought young, promising teachers to meet the university's immediate needs, but also because he regarded faculty recruitment and development as the first and foremost step in quality education. During his five years as president of DSTC and provost of UMD, he hired many notable faculty members, who, during long-standing careers, developed the curriculum and contributed to the growth of UMD. His faculty recruits included Valworth R. Plumb, Ward Wells, Ruth E. van Appledorn, Richard O. Sielaff, Henry J. Ehlers, Arthur E. Smith, John E. Verrill, Thomas W. Chamberlin, Lyda C. Belthuis, and Chester W. Wood.

Three other Gibson recruits—John E. King, Raymond W. Darland, and Robert L. Heller—collectively headed UMD for thirty-seven years. Gibson speaks with pride of the successors who carried on his struggle to build an impressive campus and turn UMD into an educational and cultural center.

Oral history interviews with retired faculty strongly suggest that many faculty members from the early days of UMD cared deeply about the

Dan Devine, UMD football captain, pinned a corsage on JoAnne Devine, his wife and Homecoming queen, in 1947. Dan Devine, a charter member of the UMD Hall of Fame, went on to become head football coach at Notre Dame, and the University of Missouri. He also coached the Green Bay Packers.

Below: Provost Raymond Gibson, right, awarded Allen Willman the prize for best float in the 1947 Homecoming parade.

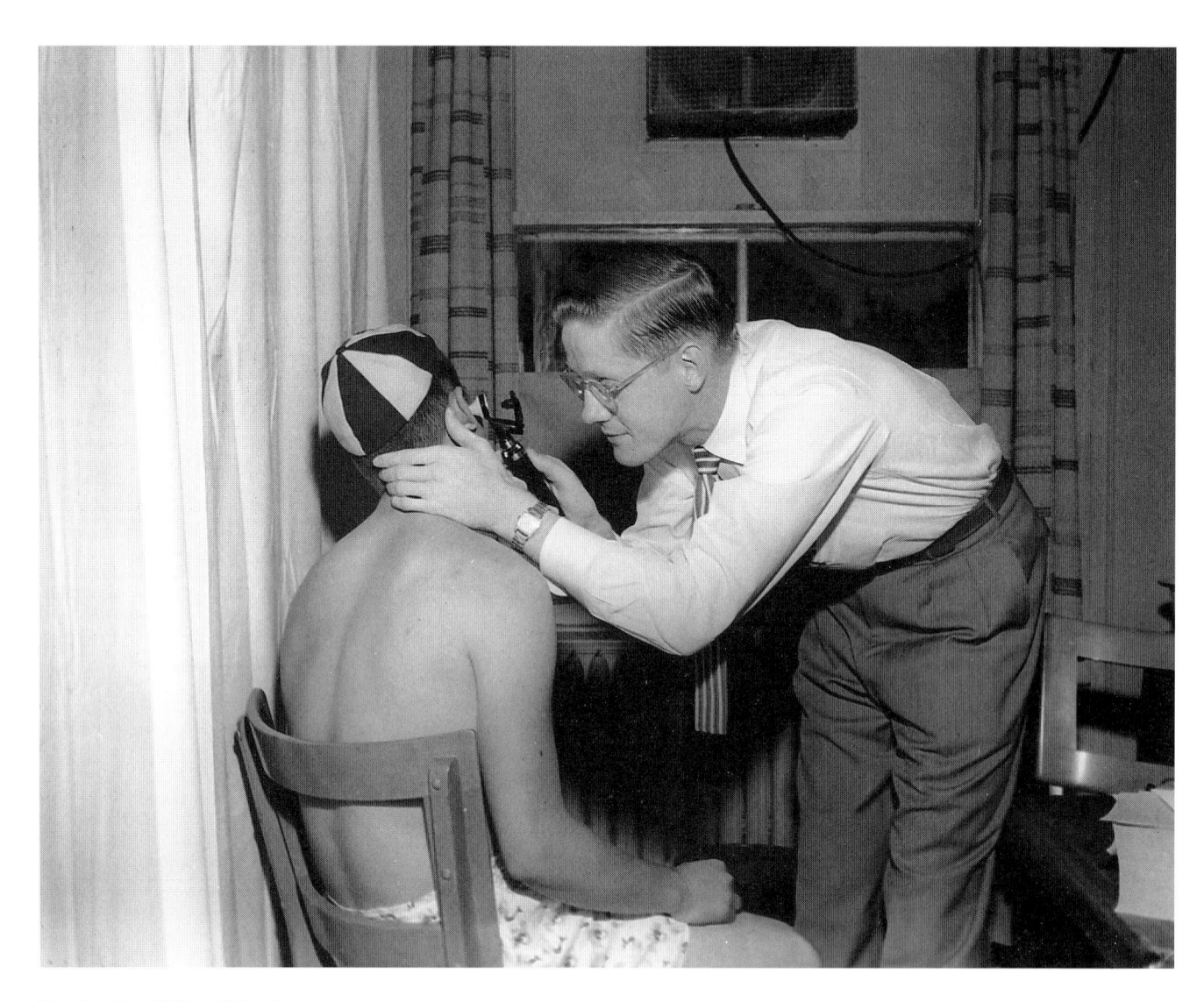

During the 1950s, all freshman students at UMD endured numerous tests during the mandatory physical exams.

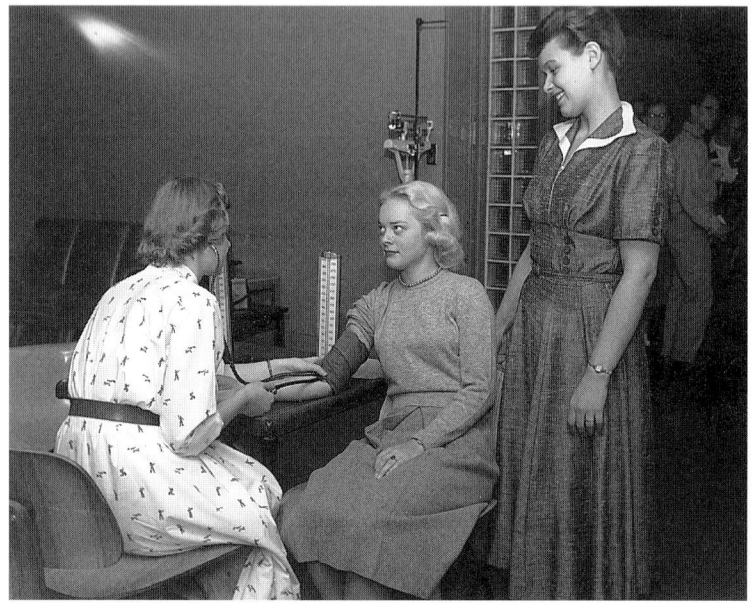

The U.M.D. Faculty

— presents —

E. Pluribus Unum*

An eight act fantasy lifted from a freshman English theme and prepared for the stage by **honorable** members of the staff.

IN 4 ACTS AND TOO MANY SCENES

McBiffle Auditorium**
DULUTH BRANCH

8:15 p. m.   May 18, 1951

* Mer Gront er Gresset Ingensteds

** The large auditoriums up on the new campus are being used for more important activities tonight — why aren't you there?

The late Professor Emeritus Thomas Chamberlin (lower left) was a professor of geography from 1947 to 1982. "We had one movie projector on campus when we started out. One day Dr. Gibson and Dr. King came over and asked if I could spend $200 before the next morning... so I went out and bought the first department movie projector for our campus," he recalled. Chamberlin and other faculty members weren't afraid to show off their non-academic talents either. "In the early Fifties, we put on some crazy things for the students," Chamberlin remembered. "We used to have a faculty show.... Bob Pierce and I did a skit of 'Me and My Shadow' doing a tap dance."

Blues guitar legend Leadbelly posed with UMD students before his campus concert on November 17, 1948.

school and are very proud today to have played a role in UMD's growth and development. Their commitment to the school was an indispensable factor in the creation of a comprehensive university campus in Duluth.

Gibson found that the University of Minnesota name was a decided advantage in recruiting first-rate faculty. Being a branch campus of a well-known university lent considerable prestige to his small institution and helped dispel the clouded reputation left in the wake of the Sorenson affair.

Provost Gibson quickly learned, however, that the connection with the University of Minnesota, while an asset in recruiting, was fraught with difficulties and imperiled his plan for a major university in Duluth. To realize his dreams, Gibson needed money. But all too quickly he learned that the University of Minnesota central administration did not share his vision for the future of UMD. Problems soon developed. As a teachers college, Duluth State had direct access to the State Teachers College Board and competed for funds as an equal with the other teachers colleges. As a branch campus of the University of Minnesota, UMD did not have direct access to the Board of

Regents and had to compete with the Minneapolis campus. UMD's budget was now controlled by its chief competitor.

Gibson reported that the Duluth campus could operate freely within its budget, but that central administration limited its funding to that of a "third-rate provincial college." Determined to build a major university in Duluth, the enthusiastic young provost was frustrated. His stormy relationship with central administration finally led to his resignation in 1950. In a 1990 oral history interview, Gibson ventured the opinion that, if the University of Minnesota central administration had treated Duluth as generously as the State Teachers College Board had treated St. Cloud and Mankato, all the state universities in Minnesota would be part of the University of Minnesota today.

Another conundrum developed when University officials demanded that all DSTC faculty be reranked in accordance with University standards, thus creating an embarrassing situation that could easily have exploded into a public controversy. The provost, with the assistance of a faculty committee, assigned tentative ranks which were reviewed by Vice President for Academic Administration Malcolm Willey and the Duluth Advisory Committee. The Advisory Committee of Minneapolis vice presidents and deans had enormous influence on UMD's development even though it had no Duluth members. A recommendation on individual faculty ranks was finally sent to the president with final approval by the Board of Regents.

Most faculty members did retain their former academic ranks, but the new requirement of a doctorate for an associate or

Provost Raymond Gibson hired Professor Emeritus Richard Sielaff to head the new Department of Business Administration at UMD in 1947. Sielaff remained a strong force in the growth of UMD's business programs until his retirement in 1985.

Provost John King was an associate professor of education when he became head of UMD in 1950.

Art students, circa 1951, find comfortable places to paint in the entry to Tweed Hall purchased and given to DSTC in 1941 by Alice and George Tweed. Tweed Hall and Olcott Hall, across the street, housed the college's art and music departments.

full professorship did lead to demotions and bitterness. Little emphasis was placed on research and publications in reranking faculty for, as Willey explained, Duluth was a teaching-oriented campus. With this painful episode etched in his memory, Gibson stated that anyone who tried to rerank faculty today would be run out of town. Still, despite some residual bitterness, most faculty remained at UMD and eagerly assumed the challenge of building a new campus and developing a curriculum suitable for a university.

Much had been achieved during Gibson's tenure and important foundations were laid for the future. Provost Gibson established a solid working relationship with Alice Tweed, a great patron of the arts. Tweed (later Tweed Tuohy) was a generous friend of UMD, donating the family's vast collection of art in honor of her recently deceased husband George Tweed, a leading Duluth financier and avid collector of the nineteenth-century French landscape painters known as the Barbizon

School. This important collection was housed on the first floor of the Tweed mansion, which was also donated to the university. Thanks to Alice Tweed, UMD became a cultural center in its early years. Fortunately, this was only the beginning of the Tweed family's beneficence.

Another milestone was the construction of the Science Building, the first structure on the Nortondale or upper campus. On January 1, 1949, Provost Gibson, speaking for all Duluthians who had fought so long and hard for the creation of a branch campus, declared, "As the new Science Building silhouette rises on the Duluth horizon, citizens of this region will know with certainty that the dream of a quarter century has come to life."

Gibson, who had achieved so much in the five critical years that he served DSTC and UMD, resigned in June 1950. Continuing his distinguished career in education, Gibson served the international community as director of the United States education mission in Peru, developing rural schools and planning a teachers college; and as director of the educational missions branch of the U.S. Office of Education, recruiting American educators to serve abroad. Peru recognized his accomplishments with a distinguished service decoration. From 1955 to 1976 Gibson served as professor of higher education at Indiana University and conducted important educational studies to assist foreign universities.

Until the Duluth Entertainment and Convention Center was built in 1966, UMD hockey players practiced and held their home games in the Duluth Curling and Skating Club on London Road. During their first several seasons, the Bulldogs played in the Duluth Amphitheater in downtown Duluth. Photo courtesy of *Duluth News-Tribune*.

Professor Emeritus Theron O. Odlaug, biology, joined the DSTC faculty as a recruit of President Herbert Sorenson in 1945. He served as Department of Biology head from 1954 to 1978, when he retired. "We had to walk what the students called the 'Yukon Trail' . . . nobody ever plowed out anything for anybody . . . we walked in hip-deep snow from the highway to the door," Odlaug said about the trek from Old Main on the lower campus to the Science Building on the upper campus in 1950. Odlaug embodied the enthusiasm of the DSTC-UMD faculty members for their chosen occupation. "Meeting with students and being able to teach was my greatest satisfaction. There wasn't a day that I got up and didn't want to go to the University to teach—not once in thirty-two years," he said.

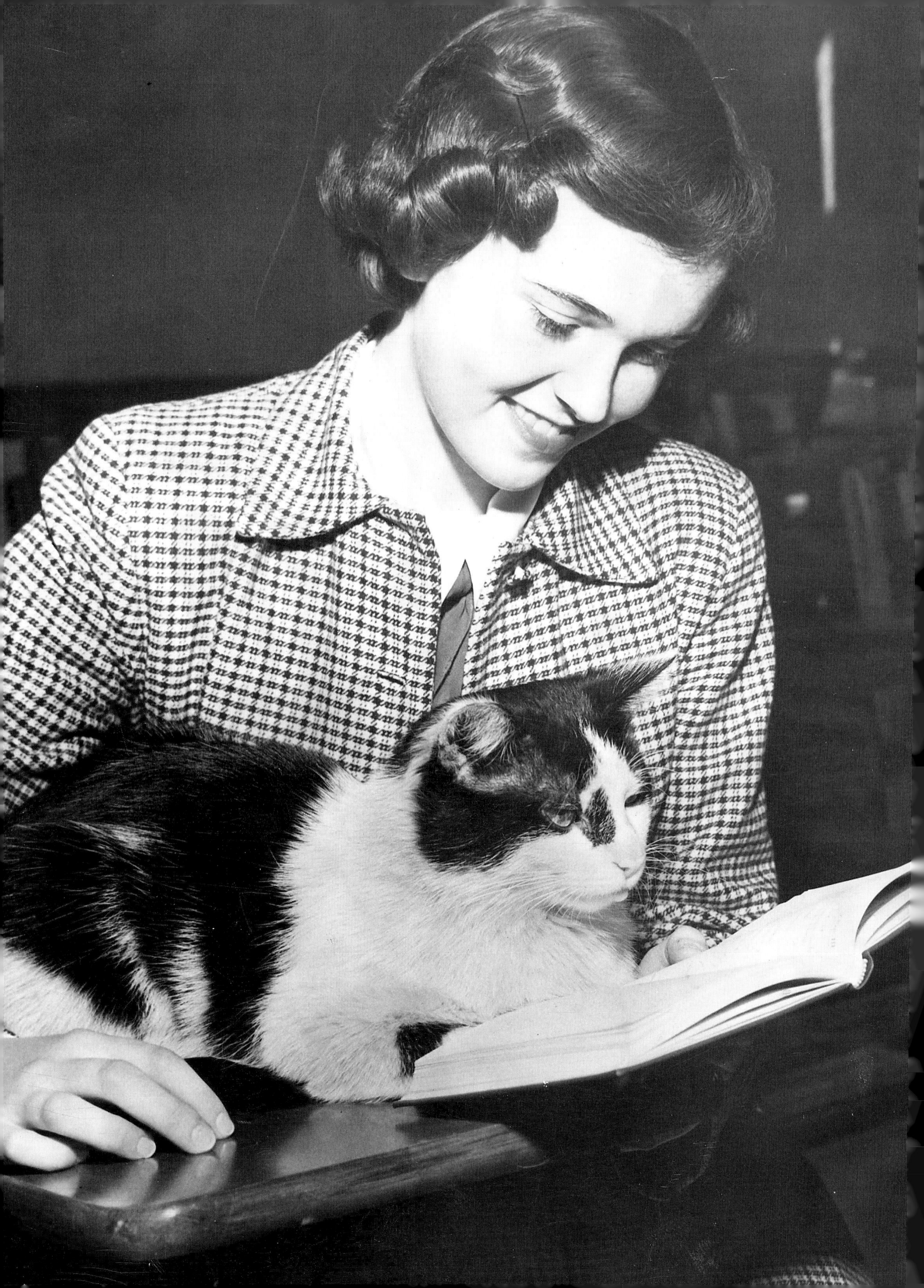

1951 Homecoming Queen Rose Hable was crowned by Ron Weber, Homecoming chair.

Left: Freshman student Sybil Wainstock studied with the help of a friendly companion in 1951.

Gibson still follows UMD events with interest. He delivered the summer commencement address in 1960 and in 1990, at the age of eighty, he returned for a nostalgic visit with former colleagues and a reception held in his honor. Gibson is indeed proud of UMD and the public-spirited citizens of northern Minnesota who have supported it.

After Gibson resigned, John E. King, academic dean and associate professor of the Department of Education, became acting provost in 1950 and provost in 1951. King, who received his Ph.D. from Cornell University in 1941, had experience as a teacher, coach, principal, and World War II naval deck officer aboard the U.S.S. *Hyde* in the South Pacific. The new provost worked tirelessly to fulfill Gibson's vision of an important university in Duluth. Mrs. King once said that her husband had only one occupation and one hobby—UMD. His enthusiasm was

Professor Emeritus Pershing "Jack" Hofslund, biology professor at UMD from 1949 to 1982, is a nationally recognized ornithologist and originator of the hawk counting survey at Hawk Ridge, an annual event which still draws birdwatchers from all over the country. Hofslund was called to Duluth for an interview in the summer of 1949. "It was ninety-six degrees in Ann Arbor, Michigan . . . at a stopover in Chicago, it was one hundred degrees in the shade," he recalled. "When I arrived in Duluth, I saw people walking around in topcoats . . . that's one of the reasons I decided to come here."

Duluth's wildlife, very much a part of campus life, also attracted Hofslund. "It was wild up here [at the upper campus] in the early '50s. Short-eared owls used to nest in a swamp where the Physical Education Building is now. Ruffed grouse and woodpeckers nested here too. We trapped the first porcupine for our collection on what is now the Chemistry Building parking lot. It was convenient for me because I did my research right here on campus," he said.

The 1952 "Buckhorn Musical Review," sponsored by the Department of Music, was performed on the Old Main stage in 1952. Music alumni adopted the "Buckhorns" name for their alumni group.

Beta Phi Kappa's 1952 float displayed its Homecoming spirit.

Phil Smith played the title role in UMD's 1952 production of *Dr. Faustus*.

Below: Director and Professor Harold Hayes, right, instructed Herb Taylor for the 1952 production of *The Importance of Being Earnest*.

Professor Emeritus Allen Downs retired in 1982 after thirty-five years as a music professor at UMD. He sang the national anthem at UMD hockey games for twenty-six years. As shown here, Downs led a UMD choral performance in the 1950s.

Right: The U.S. Air Force authorized a Reserve Officers Training Corps (ROTC) unit for UMD in 1948. ROTC sponsored the annual "Sweetheart of the Corps" event. Mary Ann Ehlers, center, was the 1952 Sweetheart, with Janet Nelson, right and Shirley Leiviska, left, as her attendants.

shared by many faculty members; home from the war, they were anxious to begin their delayed careers and threw themselves enthusiastically into the opportunities afforded by a new and expanding campus.

A group of northern legislators also responded to the challenge. Realizing that UMD needed a library and a student center, the northern delegation fought for expanded facilities in the 1953 legislative session. Minnesota lawmakers, impressed by the enthusiasm of the northern delegation and its commitment to UMD, voted to appropriate $1.1 million.

The funds were not adequate for the construction of the student center, but the St. Louis County Board of Commissioners, reflecting the county's pride in UMD, levied a special property tax to help finance the project. The rest of the money would be raised through donations. Once again, the civic and political leaders of northern Minnesota had fought for UMD and won.

Professor Emeritus Albert "Bill" Tezla, English, came to UMD in 1949 and taught until 1983. He is an internationally renowned scholar and translator of Hungarian literature. "The educators who arrived at UMD in the late '40s were challenged to develop the institution into a great one," he said. "Having survived the Great Depression and World War II, we were service-oriented and hungry for creativity. Our primary task was to take the teachers college curriculum and develop it into a university curriculum.

"My life was the classroom . . . everything I thought about or felt had its bearings on what happened in the classroom. I felt it a privilege to be with the students, and they sensed that the purpose of my teaching was to be a middle person between a great work of literature and the students. My own personal fulfillment in thirty-three years of teaching was carrying out that process."

Tezla is particularly proud of his role in developing opportunities for physically disabled students, including UMD's first non-ambulatory student, a young man in a wheelchair. "The problem was, how were we going to get him from classroom to classroom, with four floors and no elevator," Tezla recalled. "I went to the 'M' Club and I explained to those young men what the problem was and they set up a program to be at the classroom door whenever Clarence got out of class. They carried him to Washburn Hall and up to Torrance Hall . . . they even took him to the prom."

The need to carry wheelchair-confined students up and down the stairways at Old Main influenced Provost John King to include provisions for students with disabilities in the master campus plan which was unveiled in 1951.

The Albert Tezla Scholar/Teacher award is given annually to an outstanding faculty member for teaching and scholarship in the College of Liberal Arts or the School of Fine Arts.

Students enjoyed beautiful spring weather on the Old Main campus in the mid-1950s.

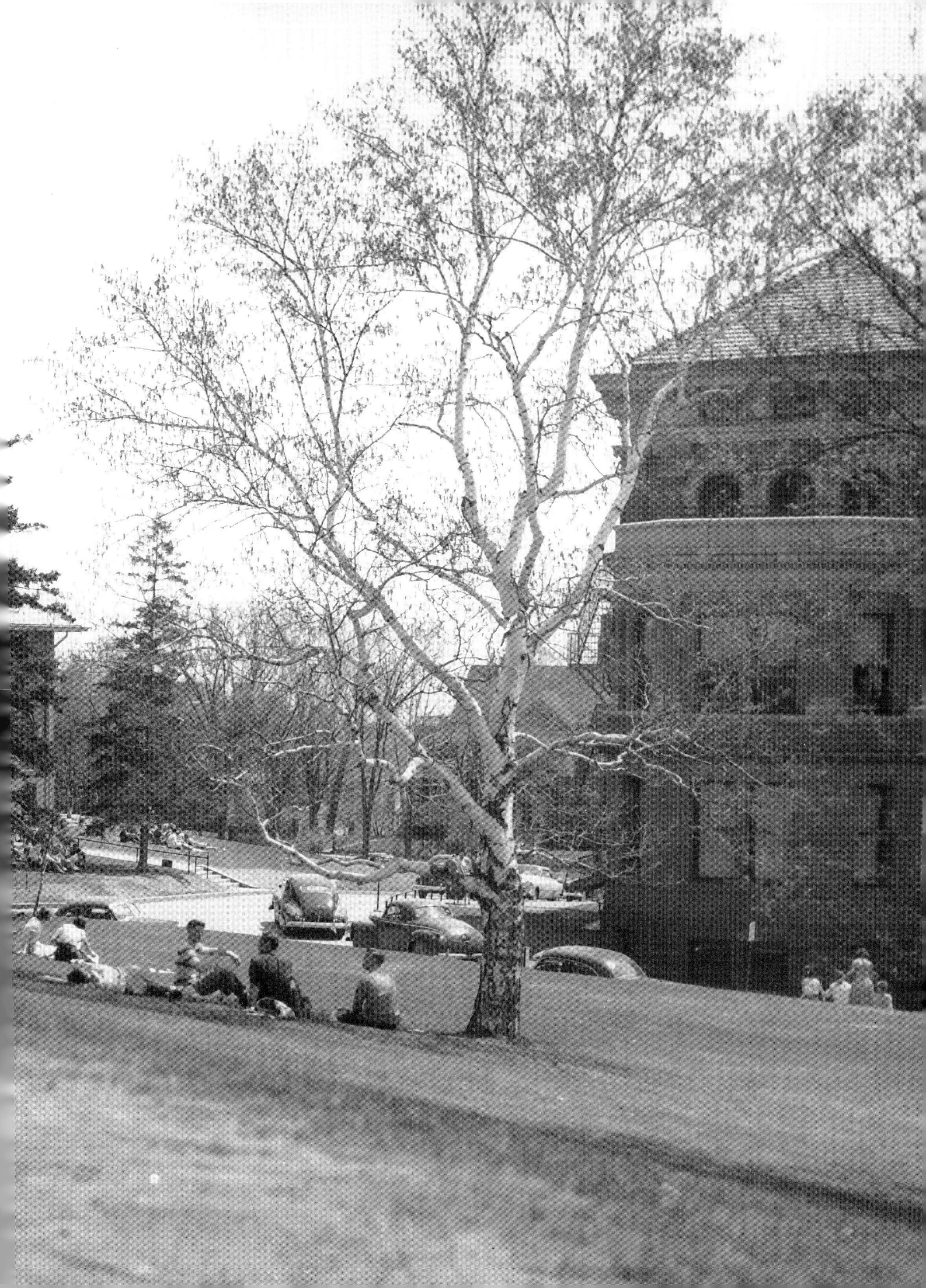

Professor Elliot Weinberg, physics, taught a night class in 1952.

The year 1953 also saw another important addition to the campus. Dr. and Mrs. William R. Bagley and their daughter, Dr. Elizabeth C. Bagley, donated a tract of land for a nature center. This tract, added to the parcel given by Charles K. and Gilbert G. Dickerman Real Estate Company and the tax-forfeited property donated by the City of Duluth and St. Louis County, provided the land for the beautiful Bagley Nature Area. Countless students and faculty have walked the trails in its cathedral-like forest, observed its wildlife, and have viewed the panoramic vista of Duluth, UMD, and the North Shore from the top of Rock Hill.

Much had been achieved during the Gibson and King years and UMD, thanks to their leadership, was ready to expand both its curriculum and physical plant. When King resigned to assume the presidency of Kansas State Teachers College in Emporia in 1953, Duluthians could reflect on the vast changes in public higher education since the end of World War II. Growing from a teachers college, with a fall 1945 enrollment of 340 students and a tiny campus of less than a dozen acres with no room for expansion, UMD had a fall 1953 enrollment of 1,395 students and a spacious campus of about 196 acres with two new buildings, Science and Physical Education. More buildings were on the way.

The Duluth community learned on November 10, 1951, that the 1948–49 campus plan of detached buildings in a semi-circle had been abandoned. Not suitable for northern Minnesota's harsh winters, it was replaced with an all-weather design. The new campus plan enabled students to go to all the major buildings under roof-covered corridors that connected the structures. The plan, worked on by a special Duluth Branch committee chaired by Winston A. Close, University advisory architect, produced a campus especially friendly to the physically impaired. UMD now had a feasible plan and community support. The next provost, Raymond W. Darland, was determined to turn the campus plan into bricks and mortar.

Right: In 1953, UMD students checked their mailboxes in Old Main. Weekly information about campus events and the *UMD Statesman* supplemented mail from the outside world.

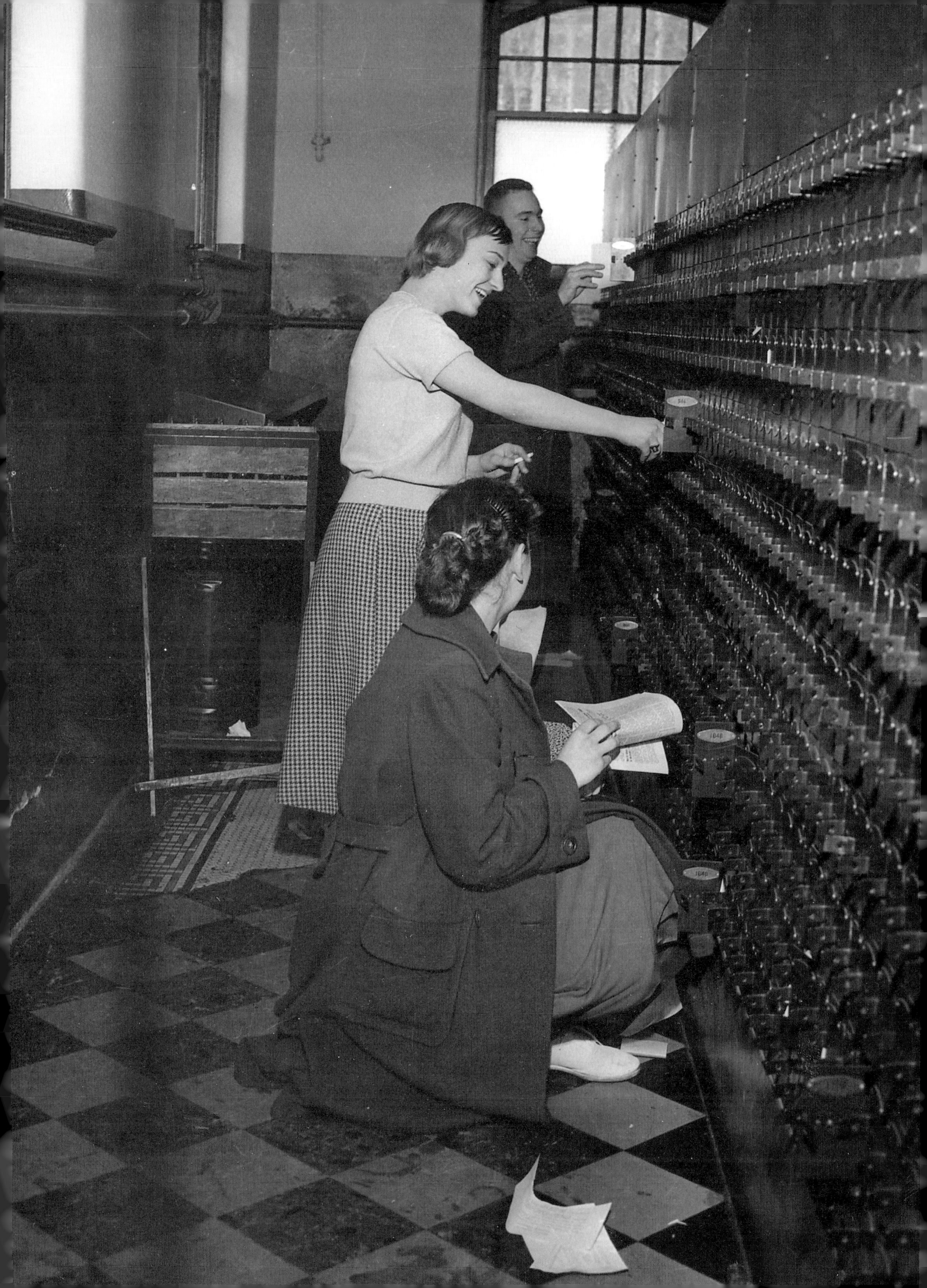

Professor Emeritus Julius F. Wolff, professor of political science from 1949 to 1986, is an authority on wilderness management and the recognized "dean" of Lake Superior shipwreck historians. As a youth, Dr. Wolff roamed the Nortondale Tract, site of the present campus. "The Zenith City Dairy [stood] where the present Physical Education Building stands. I was wandering through a fenced-off area where they had a big bull . . . and I guess I had a red jacket, or something, because the bull suddenly became very friendly and I took off over the fence leaving half of my jacket in the fence."

As an educator, Wolff's goal was to prepare students to take their places in the world: "You furnish a respectable collegiate experience to thousands of students who might not have had that experience . . . and you give them a quality bit of training so that they grow up to become creditable citizens of our community."

His Lake Superior research started out as a "project" and transformed itself into an enduring passion. "The shipwreck project opened a whole new world to me. It taught me to study the entire history and geography of Lake Superior and also brought me into contact with all types of people whom I ordinarily never would have met—from Boy Scouts to senior citizens," he said.

Student Paul "Count" Vesterstein, left, registered with the assistance of his advisor Harold Hayes in 1952. Vesterstein, a native of Estonia, moved to Duluth after leaving a displaced persons camp in 1949. He began classes at UMD in 1950. "It was tough at first with the language," he recalled. "I had a dictionary in one hand, a textbook in the other, and I tried to figure out what I was doing." Vesterstein is an active UMD alumnus and Duluth business leader.

University President James Morrill presented Kay Onsgard with a piece of cake to celebrate the University of Minnesota system's 102nd anniversary in 1953.

Left: Professor James Glick, of science and mathematics, offered advice to students during registration.

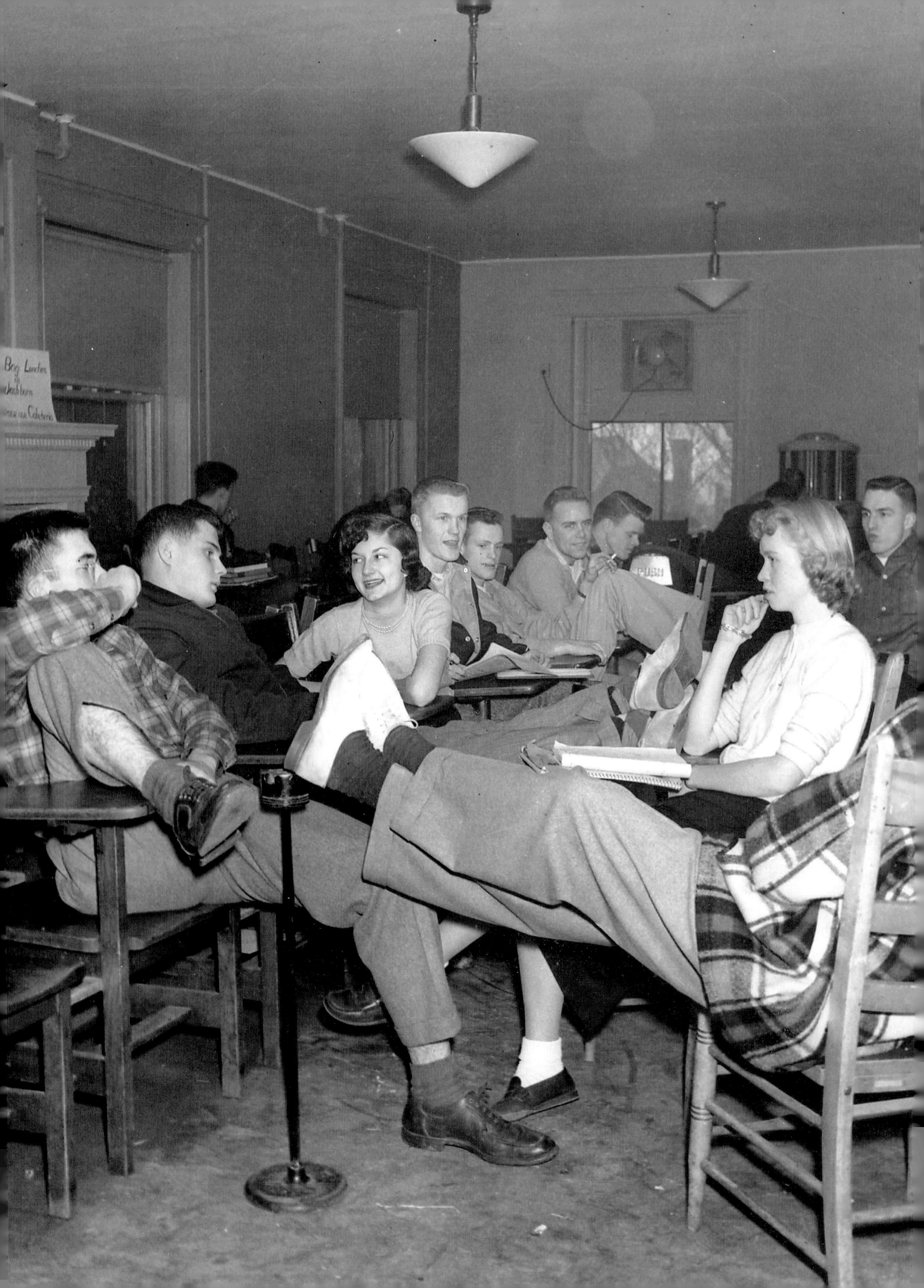
PUSH

Groundbreaking ceremonies for the Physical Education Building were held on July 12, 1951. From the left, Lloyd Peterson, Elizabeth Graybeal, Lou Rickert, and Regent Richard Griggs watched Provost King start the crane. The building was completed in 1953.

University Regent Griggs, left, and future UMD Provost Raymond Darland examined the plans for the campus expansion in 1952.

Left: Students relaxed between classes in the student lounge of Washburn Hall.

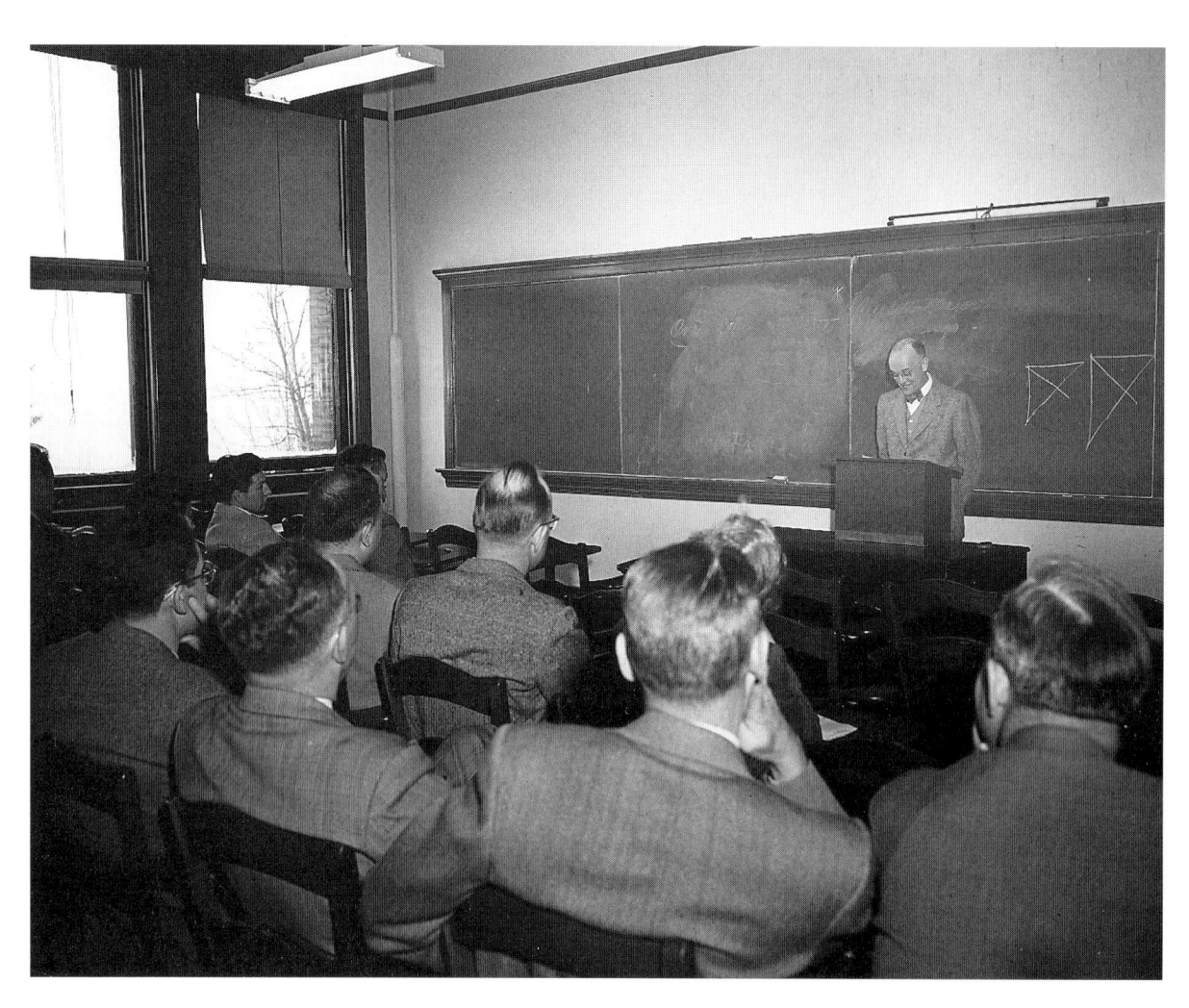

Malcolm M. Willey, vice president of the University of Minnesota, addressed the UMD faculty in 1952.

Ruth Parker and Bob Leestamper admired the gifts which were admission tickets to the annual Charity Ball of 1952.

Bandleader Ray Anthony, originator of the "Bunny Hop," and his band provided the music for the 1953 Junior Prom.

Statesman reporter Gene Gruba interviewed literary wit Ogden Nash during Nash's May 1953 visit to UMD.

Provost Raymond W. Darland, captured in a contemplative moment, guided UMD through more than two decades of building the campus and of developing the university's varied undergraduate and graduate programs.

UMD COMES OF AGE: THE DARLAND YEARS

1953–1976

Raymond W. Darland, the man who built most of the UMD campus, became provost in September 1953. He was tall—over six feet—and broad-shouldered with an engaging personality. He radiated friendliness and energy. Many still remember his

CHAPTER FOUR

vigorous handshake, quick smile, charisma, integrity, dedication, and love of UMD. Darland, who received his B.S. and M.S. degrees from Fort Hays Kansas State College and his Ph.D. from the University of Nebraska, had served as a high school science teacher, coach, principal, and like Provost King, had been a U.S. naval officer in the South Pacific during World War II. Darland came to UMD to teach biology in the fall of 1948, later serving as department head and dean.

By the time he became provost, Darland had already immersed himself in UMD's vision. He had seen the Nortondale Tract when it was an open hay meadow and participated in developing the plan that guided construction. This kind, caring man knew and valued UMD faculty and staff and added a personal touch by frequently writing notes to congratulate them on their achievements. Even his critics respected him. To the community Ray Darland was UMD! With an uncanny gift for public relations, the provost projected a positive image of UMD,

Regent Richard L. Griggs and Provost Darland were hunting and fishing partners as well as an enormously influential team in developing UMD.

explaining the economic, cultural, and educational benefits of the school for the region. He effectively garnered the political and financial support needed to build the campus and develop the undergraduate, graduate, and post baccalaureate professional programs that brought UMD of age.

In building the campus, Provost Darland was indeed fortunate to enjoy the support, confidence and active assistance of Regent Richard L. Griggs, one of UMD's greatest supporters and patrons. The rapport between them paralleled the earlier Bohannon/Washburn relationship. Griggs was a highly successful businessman who served as a university regent from 1939 to 1963. He was also an important benefactor who raised and donated money to UMD. Griggs also helped UMD by securing political support from Duluth city officials and state legislators. Darland and Griggs, hunting and fishing partners, formed a powerful team that became a major force in the development of UMD.

Flanked by University Regent Griggs, left, and Provost Darland, right, Steven R. Kirby signed the 1953 agreement to help fund UMD's Kirby Student Center. Kirby gave a major gift of $400,000. At the groundbreaking ceremony on September 30, 1954, Darland declared that "We are building for generations to come, and therefore we must build well."

Alice Tweed Tuohy addressed the crowd at the dedication of the new Tweed Gallery, constructed inside the Humanities Building, on October 19, 1958. The Tweed Gallery, with its core collection of more than three hundred French Barbizon School paintings collected by George P. Tweed, had previously been housed in the former Tweed home at 2631 East Seventh Street.

Cranes and building debris were common sights during Provost Darland's era. UMD's newest building, Campus Center, has replaced this concourse, built in the early 1960s.

Though Darland's achievements as provost from 1953 to 1976 were widely recognized and respected, criticisms surfaced. Some faculty members thought the provost focused too heavily on building, that he was not an intellectual leader nurturing a "real" university. This criticism was not entirely fair. Darland realized that university-level programs were the most important element in a school's development. The provost built programs as well as buildings.

Darland found that his effectiveness with central administration declined during the administration of Malcolm Moos, University president from 1967 to 1974. The provost's friendly, outgoing personality contrasted with the more reserved administrative style of the Moos team. However, supporters managed to save Darland's position. Growth was the most salient feature of the Darland years. When he became provost in 1953, there were only two buildings on the new campus and the fall enrollment stood at 1,395. By the 1975–76 academic year, his last as provost, there were twenty-nine buildings and the fall 1975 enrollment had climbed to 6,210.

Two important ingredients in UMD's expanding mission were the growth in enrollment and the changing geographical origins of its student body. When UMD was established in 1947, it was viewed as a regional, as opposed to a statewide, campus and was expected to serve students from the nine counties of northern Minnesota: Aitkin, Carlton, Cook, Crow Wing, Itasca, Koochiching, Lake, Pine, and St. Louis. As late as the fall of 1961, 90 percent of the students enrolled came from northeastern Minnesota. Over time, UMD's appeal broadened, and by the fall of 1969 it was drawing 20 percent of its students from outside the nine-county area surrounding Duluth. A study of the fall 1969 enrollment also indicates that most of the students from outside northeastern Minnesota were from the Minneapolis-St. Paul area. Based on these new statistics, the provost declared that UMD's mission was rapidly expanding.

As more and more students were attracted from outside northeastern Minnesota, Darland began to speak of UMD as a statewide center. Darland's description was accurate. By the 1975–76 academic year, UMD was drawing more than 40 percent

John F. Kennedy, thirty-fifth president of the United States, addressed the Land and Peoples Conference in UMD's Physical Education Building on Sept. 23, 1963. Hundreds of students and community members crowded the gymnasium to hear President Kennedy's address. The UMD community mourned and flags flew at half-mast when Kennedy was assassinated just two months later on November 22 in Dallas.

Jacques Lipchitz, sculptor, created the bronze statue of Daniel Greysolon, Sieur du Lhut, unveiled at the November 5, 1965, dedication of the Alice Tweed Tuohy addition to the Tweed Gallery. The will of the late Albert Ordean, civic leader and president of the First National Bank of Duluth, funded the sculpture and Ordean Court.

of its students from outside northeastern Minnesota, most from the Minneapolis-St. Paul area. Moreover, the number of foreign students had risen to eighty-three from the countries of Bangladesh, Brazil, Canada, Cyprus, Ethiopia, Finland, Germany, Greece, Hong Kong, India, Indonesia, Iran, Japan, Lebanon, Liberia, Malaysia, Mexico, Nigeria, Panama, Portugal, South Korea, Sri Lanka, Switzerland, Syria, Thailand, Uganda, and Vietnam.

The administration, faculty, alumni, and citizens of northeastern Minnesota were anxious to see UMD grow and develop the programs and facilities appropriate for a statewide educational center. In addition to a wide range of undergraduate programs, UMD developed an impressive array of graduate and post-baccalaureate professional programs. The first graduate degree, an M.A. in education, was offered in 1953. By 1975 UMD was offering master's degrees in nineteen fields and two post-master's certificates in educational administration. In 1972 the founding of a medical school aimed at meeting Minnesota's critical shortage of primary care physicians in towns and rural areas attracted much favorable publicity and helped make the Duluth campus visible throughout the state and the nation.

The effort to establish a medical school at UMD began as a grassroots effort stemming from a chance meeting of Dr. Samuel H. Boyer, a Duluth internist, and Robert L. Heller, then assistant to the provost, on a 1966 flight from Duluth to Minneapolis. During the short flight they discussed the possibilities for a medical school at UMD, noting that the University of Minnesota in Minneapolis had the only program in the state. They both thought Duluth was well situated to train family physicians for northern Minnesota and northwestern Wisconsin. Boyer pointed out that UMD already had strong programs in the sciences and that Duluth, as a health center for the region, already had the hospitals needed to provide clinical facilities. With determination, Heller and Boyer rallied supporters and drummed up the enormous political and financial support needed to establish a medical program at UMD.

At the 1979 dedication of the School of Medicine building, Heller recalled the time and energy required to establish the school. They were, he remembered, difficult, tiring years for those deeply involved but they were also truly rewarding years. Heller reported that, starting in 1966, and continuing until the school opened, a small group of local physicians, UMD administrators, and faculty handled the planning. In addition to Boyer, Heller, and Darland, the following were active: Charles Bagley, Theron Odlaug, and Gordon Strewler. This group was later joined by local physicians Cyrus Brown, Vern Harrington,

Donald Jackson was the director of the Darling Observatory, which was willed to DSTC by Jack Darling in 1942. The observatory was replaced by the Marshall W. Alworth Planetarium.

Eric Sevareid, CBS news commentator, delivered the first Dalton LeMasurier Memorial Lecture on February 19, 1961. The lecture series honors the memory of Duluth news pioneer Dalton LeMasurier, founder of KDAL-TV.

Reinno Puumala, William Jacott, Robert Goldish, and John Thomas; and by local businessmen Warren S. Moore, Erwin L. Goldfine, Eugene McGuckin, and H. E. Westmoreland. The business community was of course aware that the economic impact of the medical school provided the equivalent of adding a new industry. Boyer was especially active. He headed the special committee of the St. Louis County Medical Society that lobbied for a medical school at UMD. The dynamic Boyer also formed the Northern Minnesota Council for Medical Education to lobby, raise money, garner local support, and formulate plans for a school that would train physicians for family practice, especially in rural areas.

To anyone who would listen, Boyer, Heller, and Darland argued that UMD, a rapidly growing part of

Professor Emeritus Frederick T. Witzig, geography, came to UMD in 1953 and retired in 1990. "I considered myself to be a part of that first generation of faculty who were privileged to be able to come to a campus within a major university system and build a school like this," Witzig said. But he had to get used to unexpected snow. "One day in May of 1954, I was running from Old Main to my office in Washburn Hall, and I was shocked to find it was snowing outside—this was something I'd never seen in Illinois."

In 1953, before UMD's "building boom," the upper campus consisted of the Science Building, woods, meadows, and the partially completed Physical Education Building.

Right: In the summer of 1954, UMD invited painter Fletcher Martin as its guest artist. He returned in 1958 for the opening of the new home of the Tweed Gallery.

the University with strong programs in biology, chemistry, and mathematics, was a logical choice for a medical school. Besides, there was adequate space on the Duluth campus for a suitable building to house the program. A medical school at UMD could also help meet the health needs of the region. Advocates pointed out that the school would enhance the medical services offered in Duluth, making the city a regional center of medical excellence which would serve northeastern Minnesota. Southern and central Minnesota were already served by outstanding medical centers, the Mayo Clinic in Rochester and the University of Minnesota Medical School and Hospital in Minneapolis. In their drive for a medical school in Duluth, the friends of UMD faced stiff competition from groups in St. Paul and Rochester who wanted to found medical schools in their cities. The campaign on behalf of UMD was greatly advanced by a 1968 statement issued by the University of Minnesota Board of Regents recommending that a medical school be established at the Duluth campus. The regents recommended that UMD offer a two-year medical school curriculum which would allow students to transfer to the Minneapolis campus to complete their M.D. degrees.

The campaign for a medical school at UMD was also strengthened by a 1969 report made by an advisory panel of national experts appointed by the Minnesota State Legislature.

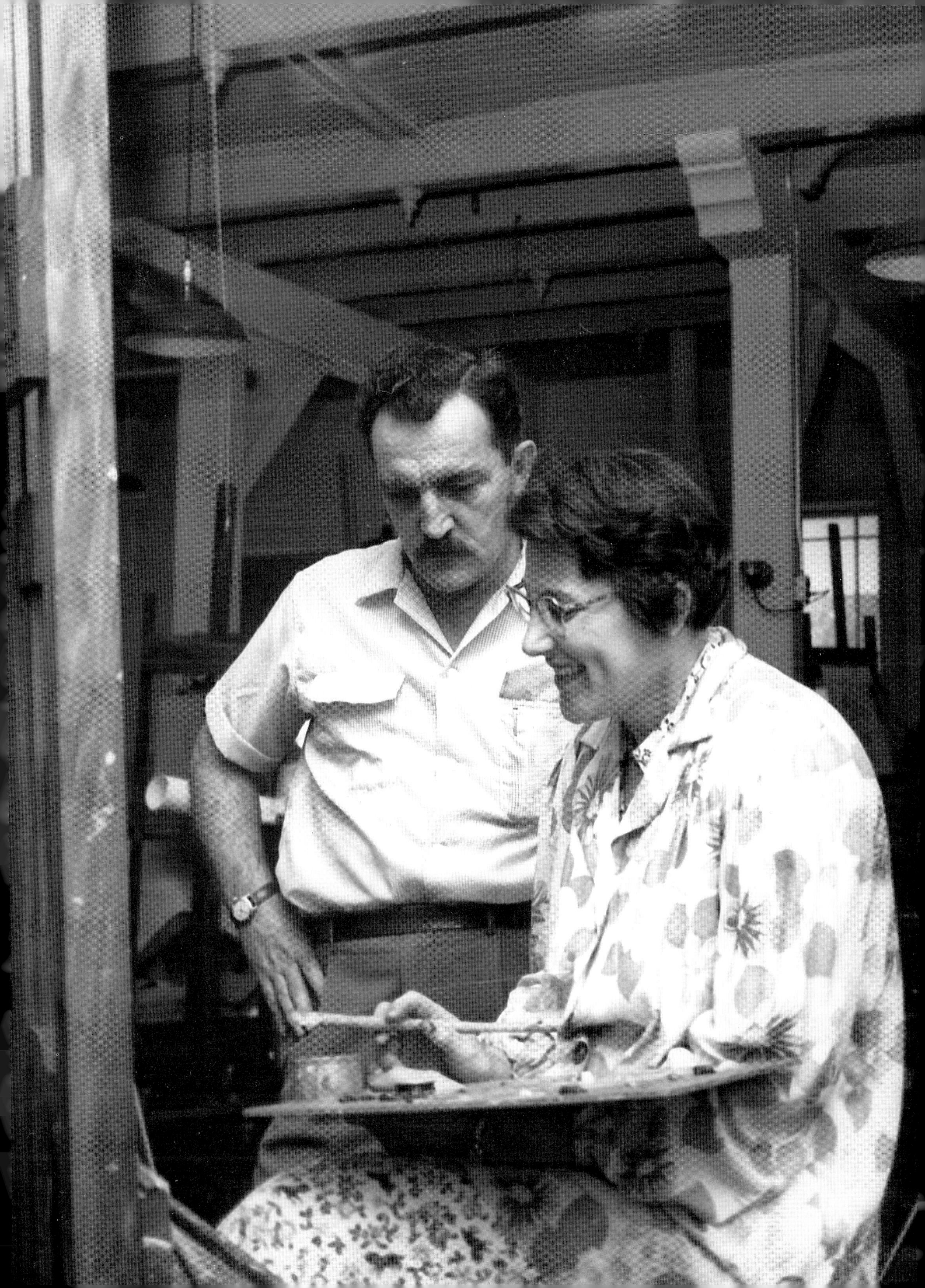

The 1954 Freshman Princess, Dona Ylinen, center, sported her beanie and her bulldog mascot. Her court included, from left to right, Pat Prevost, Margaret Ruikka, and Evelyn Rapp.

This distinguished group of five medical school deans and two medical economists was chaired by Dr. George James, dean of the Mount Sinai School of Medicine in New York City. The panel recommended that Duluth should be given first priority for a new school in Minnesota. The report of this blue-ribbon panel swayed support toward the Duluth proposal, and in May 1969 the Minnesota State Legislature authorized an initial appropriation of $340,000 for planning, curriculum development, hiring a dean, and staff recruitment. This was a big step forward for UMD, but the advocates of a medical school in St. Paul simultaneously received $200,000 for a feasibility study. Both St. Paul and Rochester remained powerful contenders. The battle continued, with UMD again aided by a prestigious report.

A 1970 report on the nation's health issued by the Carnegie Commission on Higher Education identified the Duluth-Superior area as one of nine metropolitan areas in the nation where schools should be established. The report made no

Emmett Davidson, professor of political science, was a fraternity advisor to Gamma Theta Phi. The fraternity gave him a live turkey as a Thanksgiving present in 1952.

Left: Dennis LaRoque and his future wife Arleen danced at the 1955 UMD prom.

Professor Emeritus Bob Owens, English, enjoyed a relaxing smoke outside of Washburn Hall in 1956. Washburn Hall housed some faculty offices and some student facilities.

reference to St. Paul or Rochester. The Northern Minnesota Council for Medical Education improved UMD's chances by launching a vigorous campaign to raise $500,000 in seed money. Erwin Goldfine, the drive chairman, ably assisted by Warren Moore, organized a successful campaign in 1970 that surpassed its goal. Community support was remarkable. Once again, northeastern Minnesota had rallied to support UMD. Nonetheless, strong opposition still remained in the State Legislature; some opponents clearly hoped that the UMD campaign would run out of money and energy. Not a chance! The friends of UMD persisted with their bulldog determination. The energetic campaign was assisted by Senator Hubert H. Humphrey, Congressman John Blatnik, Congressman James Oberstar, Judge Gerald Heaney, Jeno Paulucci, Regent Emeritus Fred A. Cina, and state representatives from northern Minnesota. Heller identified Minnesota legislators Alfred France, Ray Higgins, Ralph Doty, and Earl Gustafson as being particularly helpful.

In 1972 UMD's School of Medicine opened with twenty-four students taking classes in the former Laboratory School building on UMD's lower campus. Today UMD's School of Medicine has exceeded all but the most daring predictions for its success. The 1995 *U.S. News and World Report* survey, compiled from the responses of medical school deans and senior faculty, ranked UMD second in the nation in rural medicine. Recognized for training outstanding family physicians and its rural emphasis,

The new UMD Library was dedicated in February 1956. The Minnesota State Legislature designated $700,000 of a requested $800,000 for the library during its 1953 session.

Students gathered for the weekly Student Association meeting in Washburn Hall in 1956.

Left: A student waiting for registration in 1958 examined his proposed class schedule.

In 1958 Provost Raymond Darland (left) greeted former Provosts Raymond Gibson (1947–1950) and John King (1950–1953). Together, these three leaders provided the skills and the impetus UMD needed to realize its potential as a branch campus in the University of Minnesota system.

Top: Before the buildings and walkways insulating today's UMD campus were constructed, students braved the winter cold between classes.

Right: Torrance Hall was a women's dormitory in the early 1950s.

the program already has helped attract physicians to rural areas. The medical school also has effective programs related to American Indian and minority health concerns.

American Indian Studies is another important program that is linked to and serves the northeastern Minnesota region. When George F. Himango returned to Duluth from Vietnam, he was troubled by the small number of American Indian students at UMD. Indeed, only two American Indians graduated that year. With characteristic energy, Himango recruited about a dozen friends and convinced them to come to UMD, where they started to organize and work for a program in American Indian studies. Clearly, the establishment of the program was a grassroots effort by local American Indian people, American Indian students, UMD administrators, and faculty. Professors Timothy G. Roufs and David M. Smith, anthropologists with strong interests in American Indian culture, worked hard to establish the program.

The Kirby Student Center dedication and open house was held in the center on June 22, 1956. Standing in front of the plaque honoring Stephen Kirby (who had died in 1955) were Provost Raymond Darland, far left, Regent Richard Griggs, Mrs. Stephen R. Kirby, and University of Minnesota President James Morrill.

Student pool "pros" wielded their cues in the Kirby poolroom in 1958.

Professor Emeritus Wendell P. Glick, English, served UMD from 1952 to 1986. "When the students invited George Lincoln Rockwell to speak at a seminar on extremism, I was chosen to introduce Rockwell, and I wanted to get him teed off, so I introduced him as a Nazi," Glick said. "After his speech, we had questions from the audience . . . some were too tame, so I substituted some that I thought would provoke a few sparks. Ray [Provost Darland] was afraid that the students might be seduced by Rockwell, and I said, if they can be seduced by a man like that, we're not doing our job . . . I bet he [Rockwell] didn't convert a single student to Nazism.

"The greatest pleasure I got at UMD was teaching young people . . . it wasn't work to me to have a class and to try to get them to think about what it means to be a human being and then to watch them develop . . . the study of literature will do that. I think that's the most rewarding part of teaching," Glick added.

Students lingered over coffee in the Torrance Hall cafeteria in 1958.

Frederick T. Witzig, chair of the Social Science Division, later dean of the College of Letters and Science, helped the founders deal with administrative hurdles. American Indian Studies received a strong start in 1972 when Robert E. Powless, a multi-talented American Indian educator, was hired to direct the program. Powless, an outstanding teacher with a flair for public speaking, built a solid academic program that offers courses on American Indian history and culture.

Today, thanks to local American Indian people and the work of many faculty and staff at UMD, the campus has a department of American Indian Studies and an American Indian Learning Resource Center. The growth of academic programs was an important element in UMD's coming of age, but it was not the only factor. For most American educators academic freedom is not a luxury or a privilege; it is an indispensable condition of teaching and exists at the very heart of a genuine university. A university is first and foremost a community of scholars where ideas are tested by open discussion. In that view it is vital that a wide range of ideas be expressed and that speakers who represent controversial views and organizations be nonetheless welcomed on campus. Provost Darland protected academic freedom in 1965 when he decided not to overrule the Student Association's decision to invite two controversial speakers to campus, American Nazi Party leader George Lincoln Rockwell and American Communist Party leader Gus Hall.

Some civic and business leaders vehemently opposed allowing such "un-American" speakers on campus and argued that they should not be heard at a tax-supported institution. The student government's invitations also aroused the ire of Regent William K. Montague and former Regent Richard L. Griggs. So

James S. "Mo" Malosky, head football coach and professor of physical education, came to UMD in 1958. He's still head football coach, with several honors to his credit: the winningest active NCAA Division II coach in the nation; the eleventh winningest football coach in college history overall; and a four-time designee as Coach of the Year. Malosky has always put his players first. "I have always said that I've never won a game—it's been the ballplayers who have played here," he said. "Over the years, the wins and losses are memorable, but you have a tendency to put that on the back burner. The more important thing is to see the accomplishments of so many young men once they leave the program . . . to see that they have benefited from their experiences both on the field and in their classes at UMD . . . to see them become productive citizens. That's been the most gratifying part of what we've accomplished here."

Jerry Music and Myrna Johnson played the leads in the 1959 spring musical *Guys and Dolls*. Music went on to become the voice of the doorman on the 1970s television sitcom *Rhoda* and made numerous other Hollywood appearances.

confident were some in the business community that the vast majority of students did not agree with their Student Association's decision to invite the controversial speakers that they suggested a referendum, offering to pay for voting machines and clerks. The referendum was held, but the student body voted overwhelmingly in favor of hearing the speakers. Rockwell, appearing in person, spelled out for his polite, but skeptical, audience, his contention that American and European Jewish leaders had hatched a Communist conspiracy and controlled an American news media that was distorting the truth. His Nazi version of the "truth" included the notion that African-Americans should go back to Africa or live on reservations in America without citizenship.

Gus Hall, unable to attend, was represented by Arnold Johnson of New York, public relations director for the Communist Party of America. Johnson spoke in favor of socialism and attacked America's involvement in Vietnam. The entire situation was a severe crucible for Darland. Despite

Members of the Beta Phi Kappa fraternity posed with the 1960 UMD Snow Week Queen, Jeris Jerina. The HMS *Jeris* won first place in the snow sculpture contest.

At the September 14, 1960, groundbreaking of the Education Building (renamed Bohannon Hall in 1974), several UMD administrators reviewed the building plans. Pictured were, from left to right, Thomas Chamberlin, Armas Tamminen, Robert W. Bridges, Provost Darland, and Valworth Plumb.

Professor Emeritus Arthur E. Smith served as professor of art from 1949 to 1980 and was director of the Tweed Gallery from 1957 to 1969. Smith, former Tweed Gallery Curator Fred Triplett, and Alice Tweed Tuohy toured several university galleries in the Midwest to explore the possibility of building a larger museum facility on campus. "The Tweed Museum of Art has been the number one unit of the University that brings the town and gown together," Smith said. "I'm very proud of my part in bringing internationally known artists such as Yasuo Kuniyoshi, Max Weber, Arnold Blanch, Fletcher Martin, Philip Evergood, Dong Kingman, and Will Barnett to UMD for summer workshops."

"As the years went by, the price of art went up and it was harder to get them, but we had some fantastic people here and no other school in the country had a program like this. It gave a heritage to the whole art program here that still continues."

Mike Berman, UMD student and 1960 Homecoming chairman, wore a raccoon coat and UMD beanie. With necessary megaphone in hand, Berman cheered for a Bulldog victory.

In October of 1960, Mrs. Alice Tweed Tuohy was the first woman awarded the University of Minnesota Regents Award. Standing beside Mrs. Tuohy were Regent Griggs, left, and Dr. Edward L. Tuohy, her second husband and co-founder of the Duluth Clinic.

intense pressure from the business community that UMD depended on so heavily for support and his own patriotic views, Darland stood firm. Academic freedom prevailed! Regarded by some as just a "bricks and mortar" provost, Darland defended one of the most basic tenets of a genuine university in the face of severe community pressure.

An array of outstanding, if less controversial, speakers also characterized the Darland years. Among them were President John F. Kennedy, who spoke two months before his assassination in November 1963; Arthur Schlesinger, Jr., Pulitzer Prize-winning historian and Kennedy adviser; B. F. Skinner, Harvard professor of psychology and leading exponent of behaviorism; Carl Rogers, Wisconsin professor of psychology and psychiatry, well known for his client-centered approach to therapy; Arnold Toynbee, noted English historian and author of the twelve-volume *Study Of History*; W. H. Auden, Pulitzer Prize-winning poet; William O. Douglas, associate justice of the U.S. Supreme

The men of Beta Phi Kappa purchased the first fraternity house in UMD history in 1961. Beta members displayed their "frat house" sign at 1919 East Second Street.

A converted Model T made a great Homecoming parade attraction.

Homecoming activities such as bonfires, parades, and royalty contests were adopted by DSTC in the 1930s to generate revenue from the alumni and support for the football team. These traditional activities, along with variety shows, dances, and other pre-game events, were carried over when DSTC became a branch of the University of Minnesota. Homecoming rituals were kept alive through the "glory days" of the '50s and '60s with high jinks such as trophy "borrowing" from rival teams, and dances featuring popular bandleaders like Les Elgart.

Student activism against the Vietnam War and a new awareness of environmental and social problems in the early '70s put a damper on Homecoming activities. An attempt was made to revise the tradition in the late '70s and again in the early '90s. The 1991 Homecoming featured a tailgate party (an innovation of the '80s), a dance in the Bull Pub, and the first full parade in a decade. The attempts to recapture the spirit were only moderately successful, however, and 1991 proved to be the last time UMD elected a Homecoming king and queen. By the fall of 1995, Homecoming activities other than the football game had all but disappeared. –*Jackie Moran*

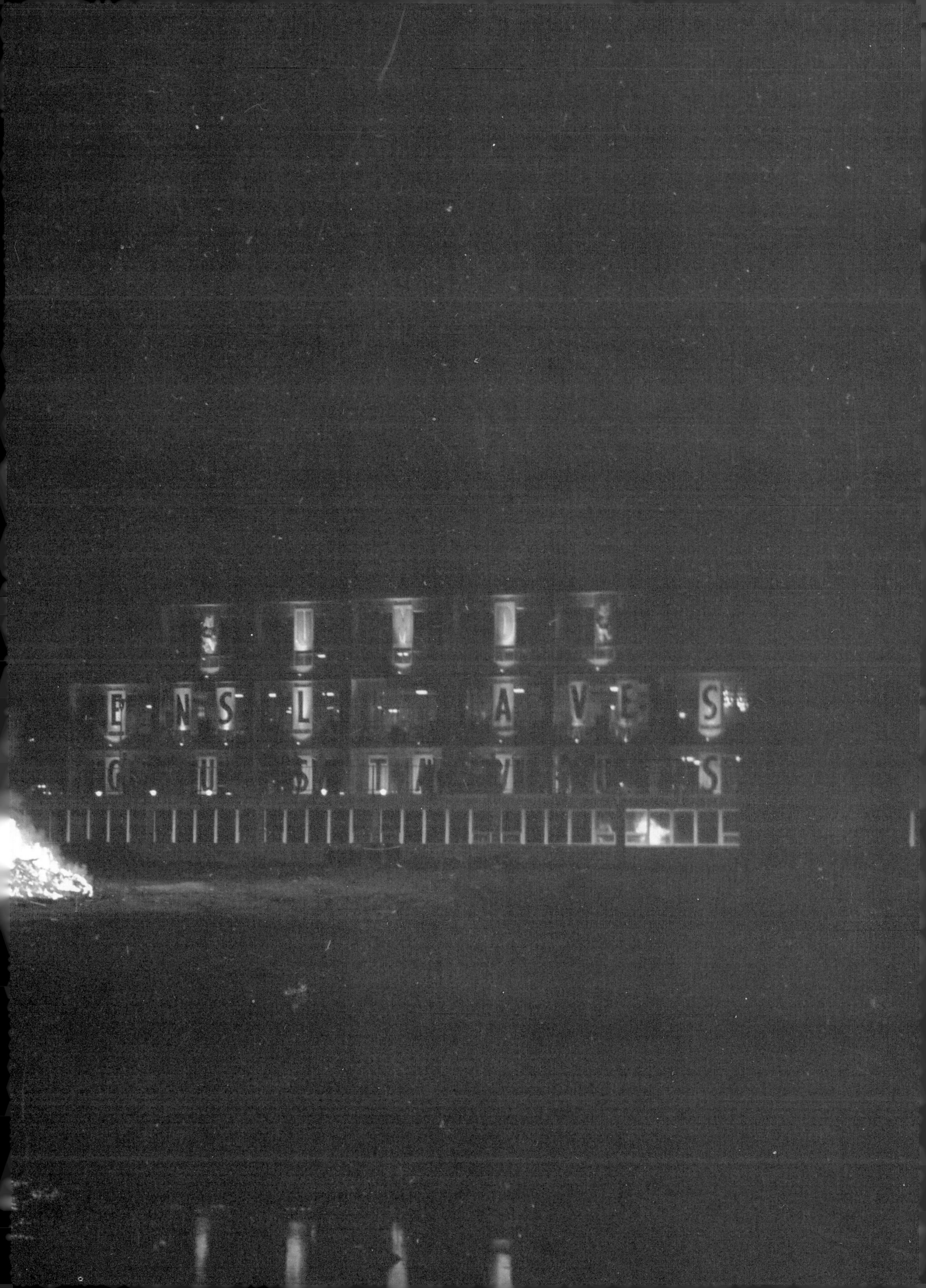

Professor Emeritus Armas W. Tamminen, psychology, served from 1952 to 1981. "When I came here, it was a family institution—everybody knew everybody," he said. He also remembered a significant milestone for UMD. "Somewhere in the '70s, two psychologists created a system for rating national graduate programs in counseling. The UMD psychology department was in the top twenty out of some four hundred—the Minneapolis campus was not! That was one of our high points."

One of Tamminen's toughest assignments was bringing B. F. Skinner and Carl Rogers, two world-renowned psychologists, to campus in June 1962. "We called Rogers and he said he'd come if Skinner was willing to come—I'm sure he thought Skinner would never come," Tamminen said. "We wrote to Skinner and he was speaking somewhere in Wisconsin and since he was going to be that close, he agreed to come. We wrote to Rogers and he was stuck. The ballroom was jammed to overflowing . . . psychologists came from all over the Midwest."

Court and prominent champion of civil rights and freedom of speech; and Senator Wayne Morse of Oregon, a leading critic of President Lyndon B. Johnson's policy in Vietnam.

Athletics, another area of growth during the Darland years, increased school spirit, attracted students, improved alumni relations, and ultimately made UMD more visible throughout the region and beyond. When thinking about the development of UMD's athletic program, especially in hockey, the name of Ralph A. Romano comes readily to mind. Romano, a UMD graduate and hockey player who earned three varsity letters as a goalie, coached the hockey team from 1959 to 1968. Though he did not lead his teams to winning seasons, he changed UMD hockey forever when he took his squad out of the Minnesota Intercollegiate Athletic Conference, scheduled games with stronger teams, and eventually gained membership in the Western Collegiate Hockey Association (WCHA), the major conference in collegiate hockey.

After leaving coaching, Romano remained to continue his work in sports administration and to become UMD director of athletics. In the early 1970s, he was instrumental in developing the women's athletic program. He also worked to obtain funds to renovate and expand athletic facilities. Romano continued as athletic director until his untimely death in 1983. In 1988 Romano was posthumously honored at dedication ceremonies when the Physical Education Building was renamed Romano Gymnasium.

Right: During "Rush Week," students had the chance to test out fraternities and sororities of their choice. These students were involved in Sigma Psi Gamma's 1963 rushing activities.

go sigma psi

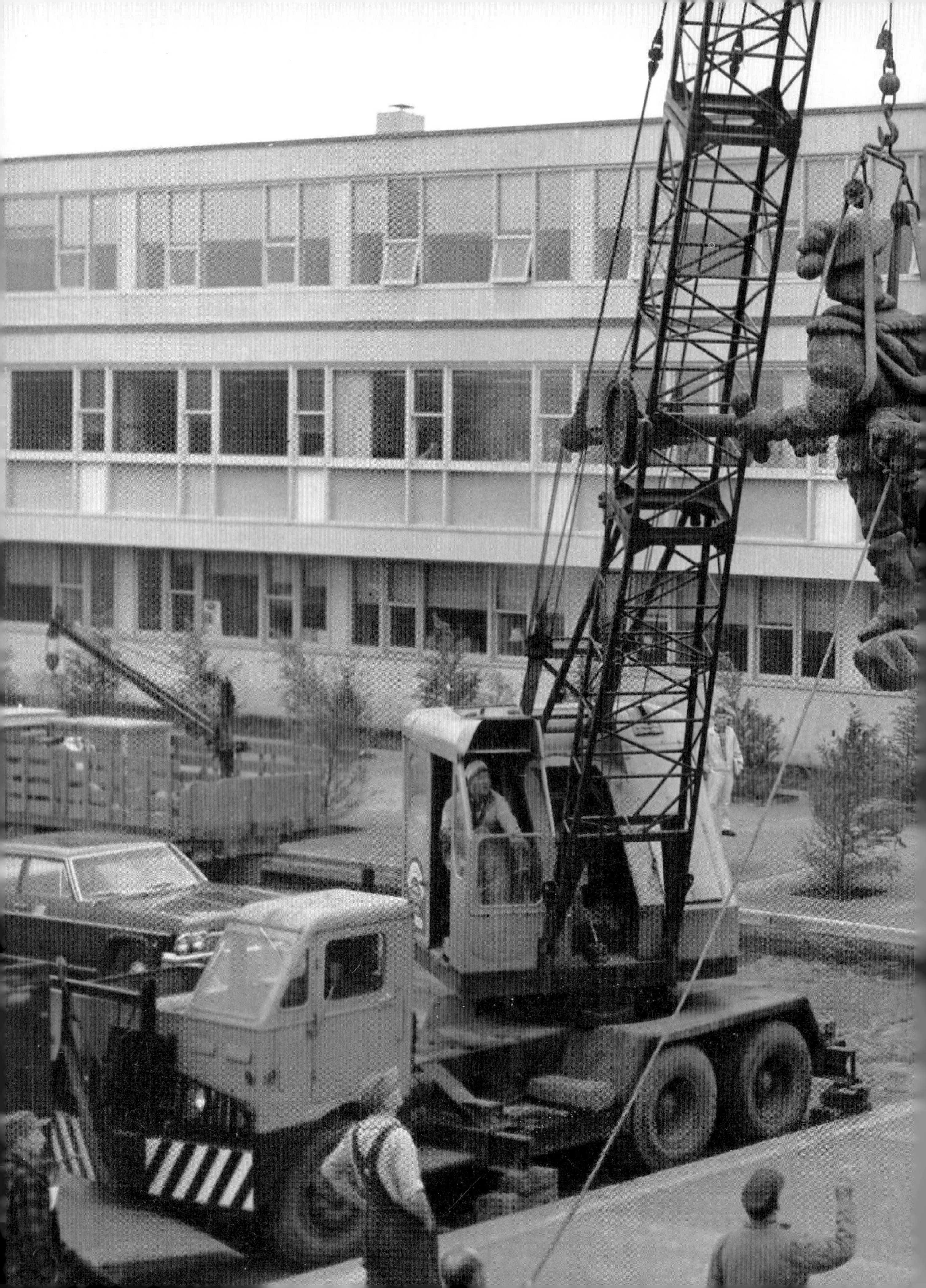

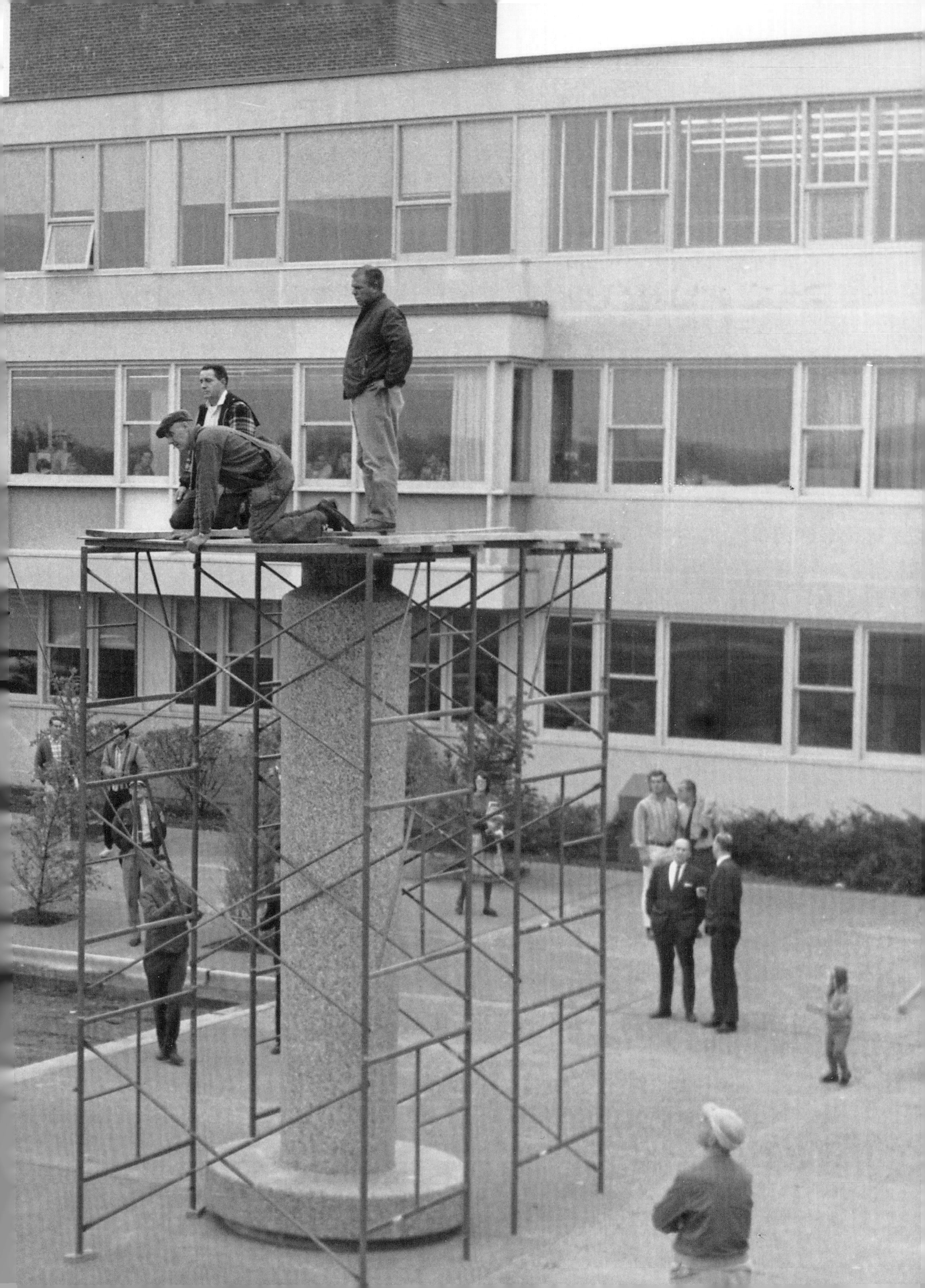

CHANGING TIMES
By Beatrice Luoma Ojakangas

Back in 1952, the University of Minnesota, Duluth Branch, was coming out of the "teacher college" mode, but still couldn't quite shake that image. John King was the provost, Ray Darland was the academic dean, and Robert Heller was the geology department. The Science Building on the "new campus" was completed and in use, and the Physical Education Building was still unfinished. A bus regularly ran from Old Main to the Science Building and four blocks down Twenty-fourth Avenue East to Olcott Hall and Tweed Hall.

I was a freshman that fall, and the major choices for "girls" were limited to education, nursing, or home economics. We joked that those who went for a B.A. degree were pretty much those who were looking for the "Mrs." degree, and never really planned to work. I wasn't particularly interested in being a teacher, but I, along with my classmates, was advised to select the B.S. in Home Economics track. "You know," they told us, "you can always 'fall back' on teaching." I really wanted to learn how to write, but because of all the education classes that interfered with English courses, it wasn't possible to schedule anything beyond the basic requirements in that department.

Haven't things changed? Home Economics no longer exists at UMD, women have become more assertive, and most students don't count on graduating in four years.

For three of my four years, I lived at Torrance Hall, along with fifty-six other girls. Life at the dorm was made spicy by the antics of the "rangers" who found clever ways to break the curfew and dared to do it. I loved my corner room, which cost me a little more than the other rooms, $49 a month, but I was able to hold down three jobs on campus to pay for my expenses. I washed dishes in the cafeteria in the evenings and manned the coffee and snack table during lunch. Between classes, I typed for an education professor and did clerical work in the business and education office. Combined, these jobs paid me enough money so that I could even send money home once in awhile. "My $100-a-year scholarship covered tuition for three quarters, and I ended up with no student loans to my name!"

Torrance Hall was one of the four buildings on the "lower campus." Washburn Hall, which housed the health center and student offices, Old Main, where most of our classes were held, and the Laboratory School, where student teachers practiced, were the other three. Four blocks down the hill the Olcott and Tweed mansions had been converted into music and art classrooms. Tweed Annex (the carriage house to the old mansion), housed ROTC. This turned the whole neighborhood into a campus, and lots of students rented rooms in nearby private homes.

The "home" for home economics majors was on the third floor of Old Main, and we were pretty well programmed. The first course all freshman home economics majors and minors were required to take was "Personal Grooming." I nearly flunked that course because I refused to wear a girdle. Girdles gave me a *stomachache*. Besides, I had strong stomach muscles from pitching hay and doing other physical work on the home farm. I figured I had my own natural girdle. I sort of squeaked by my clothing construction courses,

"My $100-a-year scholarship covered tuition for three quarters, and I ended up with no student loans to my name!"

although it was fun to learn tailoring and how to make hats.

Food preparation wasn't nearly so advanced. We'd boil an onion for a couple of hours and "scientifically" try to figure out why it didn't have any flavor. We struggled through the typical biscuit and muffin classes, and finally planned menus. Menus were geared to help us through Home Management House, where we, as seniors, were to spend six weeks cooking, cleaning, and entertaining in the big old Alworth mansion on Sixth Street. While I was a student at Home Management House, I sewed my wedding dress, much to the displeasure of Professor Ruth Palmer, who was hoping that, instead of getting married, I would fill one of the teaching jobs that was posted on the Department of Home Economics bulletin board, so that I could "pay back my debt" to society.

Nutrition, child development, family relationships and an exhaustive list of education courses filled our schedules for four years. I enjoyed the science classes which were required—physics, biology, inorganic and organic chemistry—which I still feel taught me more about why things happen in cooking than any food preparation course ever did.

I'll never forget organic chemistry courses from Professor Fayle. "Fail with Fayle," we'd say. He would write equations on the black board with his right hand as fast as he could and erase them just as fast with his left hand. Then, he'd spin toward the class, and point to one of us, "What's been oxidized, Miss Luoma?" It was a lesson in withstanding intimidation. There were those pre-meds in the same class who knew all the answers, and Fayle knew that, so he zeroed in on the home economics majors.

There were three major social events each year. The Marriage Ball during fall quarter was where you went through a mock marriage ceremony, kissed your date in public, and then were carried through a wedding-ring threshold. (This was the first real date Dick [Richard Ojakangas] and I had, and I was terrified!) The Snow Ball, with its elected king and queen, was the winter quarter event, and Prom was in the spring. We employed the "Big Bands"—Tommy Dorsey, Glenn Miller, and Duke Ellington *live* for dance music!

Beatrice Luoma Ojakangas, B.A., home economics '56, is a nationally known food writer. She is the author of twenty cookbooks and has frequently contributed to publications such as Bon Appétit, Gourmet, *and* Cooking Light. *Her newest book is* Light and Easy Baking *published by Clarkson and Potter, a division of Random House.*

The 1963-64 *UMD Statesman* staff gathered for a yearbook photo. The *Statesman* publishes weekly except during final examinations throughout the academic year.

By the 1975–76 academic year, Darland's last, UMD men competed in eleven varsity sports—hockey, football, basketball, swimming, wrestling, skiing, track, cross-country, baseball, golf, and tennis. The hockey team competed in the WCHA and other teams competed in the Northern Intercollegiate Conference. Women's sports included field hockey, volleyball, swimming, basketball, track and field, tennis, cross-country, skiing, and softball.

Donors improved campus life by helping to make UMD an athletic and cultural center. Highly successful in securing private support, Darland believed in the "soft-sell approach to development." He explained that to raise money "you have to establish a firm friendship and atmosphere of trust. And most importantly the prospective donor has to really believe that his or her gift to UMD would enrich the campus in some way." What would UMD be like today without generous benefactors? It would be a shadow of itself. Benefactors made possible such athletic and cultural facilities as Griggs Field and Stadium, the Campus Club, Kirby Student Center, Tweed Museum of Art,

The sculpture of Sieur du Lhut has been the target of some good-natured ribbing by UMD students, who once hung a huge yo-yo on du Lhut's outstretched finger. On another occasion, students painted yellow footprints leading down the pedestal, across the courtyard, into the concourse, into a men's restroom, and back again to the top of the pedestal. As shown here the French explorer flaunted frontier sheriff stars.

Glensheen, Alworth Planetarium, Marshall Performing Arts Center, Jacques Lipchitz's statue of Daniel Greysolon Sieur du Lhut, and Ordean Court. Benefactors have been and continue to be an essential element in UMD's growth and development.

The growing maturity of UMD was recognized in 1959 when the Board of Regents unanimously voted to change the school's name by dropping the word "branch" from its title. Provost Darland and the faculty had urged the elimination of the word "branch" because it was a stigma that hindered recruitment. The UMD community was delighted by the change and all the signs with the qualification "branch" were quickly replaced. Regent Griggs was extremely pleased, declaring that the change in name reflected the growing stature of the Duluth campus. Another important step away from its teacher college and branch campus origins was a UMD reorganization plan approved by the Board of Regents in 1974: The division system left over from the teachers college was eliminated in favor of colleges and schools.

Skaters took to the ice in 1963 in front of the Kirby Student Center.

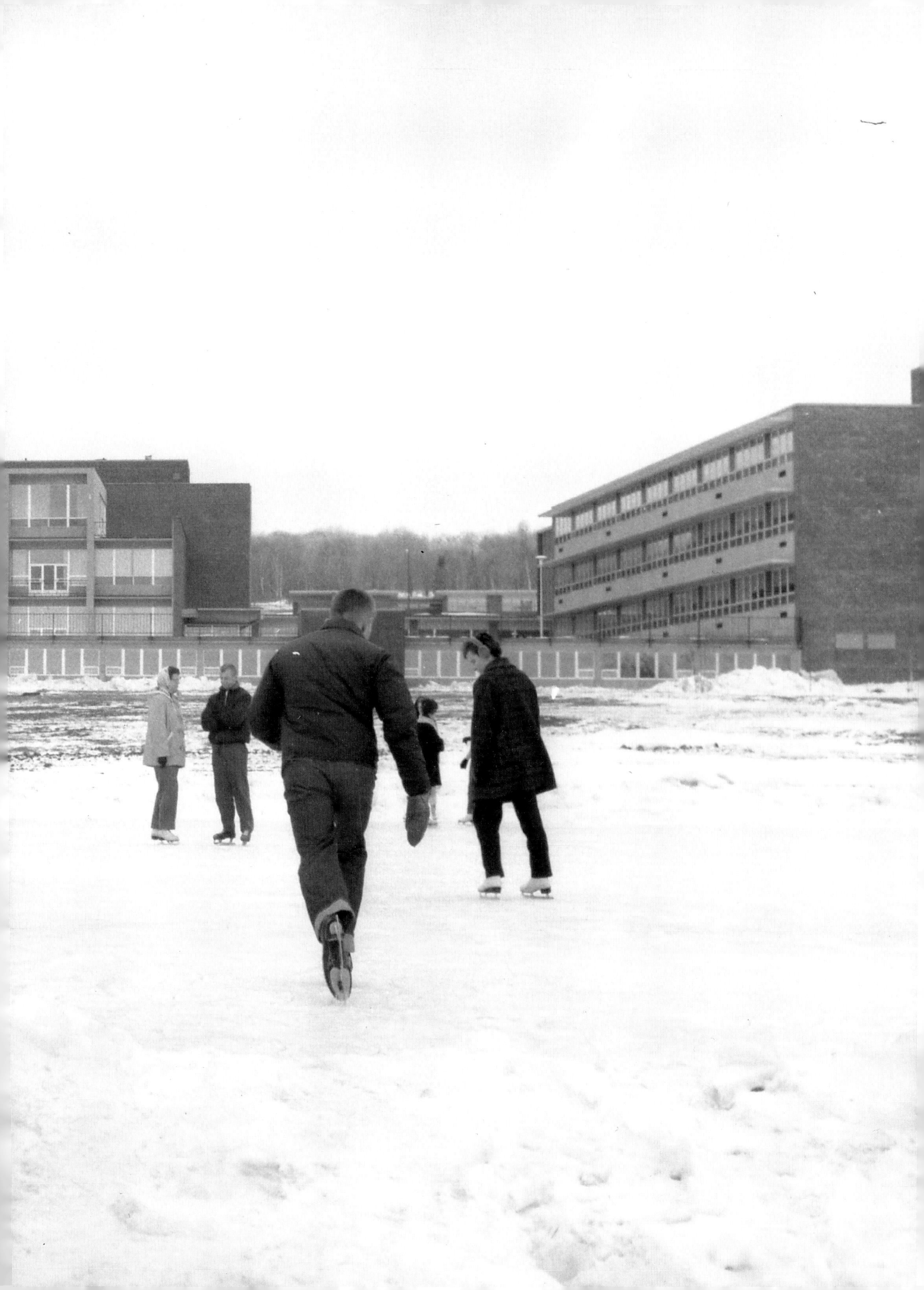

Frank McCray, B.A., English, '67 and M.A., English '71, taught English in Uganda and St. Paul, Minnesota. He was the human relations/multicultural director for the Roseville, Minnesota, public schools for thirteen years. He now owns an insurance agency in Woodbury, Minnesota.

> "A broad liberal arts education is the arm that gives flight to the heaviest object."

COMING OF AGE AT UMD
By Frank McCray

I have many vivid memories of UMD, but even those that are less clear still afford delight and shed light on my coming of age at UMD. A native Floridian, I remember the spectacle of people hurrying to Lake Superior to net thousands of little fish. I also remember my first winter, the requisite snipe hunt along the North Shore, and friends who routinely left for the weekends to go to "the lake" or "the cabin." I often wondered where "the lake" and "the cabin" were. Names like Long Lake, Round Lake, Big Lake, and Big Fork inspired little confidence after the first snipe hunt, but these forays with friends from UMD formed the beginning of lifelong friendships that still sustain me.

Some of our friendships have become extended family. Kenner, Donnan, Odin, and Anders Christensen—students at UMD—became "my brothers" and their parents, Chris and Dory Christensen, opened their home to me. I remember trying to explain to our young daughter how grandma and grandpa Christensen became her grandparents, when, out of nowhere, she wanted to know why they were Danish-Americans and we were African-Americans. After a circuitous explanation, which ended near Hinckley, she said, "That's nice." Years later, lightning struck with our son, who wanted to know if Bob and Mary Jane Owens were on my side of the family or his mother's. Before I could explain that Bob Owens was my mentor at UMD and that his and Mary Jane's enthusiasm for East Africa led to my teaching in Uganda, our then twelve-year-old daughter said knowingly, "It all started a long time ago at UMD...."

The impact of a good, liberal arts education on my professional life has been as important as the friendships developed at UMD. As an undergraduate I learned many things that still hold me in good stead. Particulars are sometimes fuzzy, but historical and intellectual currents can still be recalled. What is more important than this is the positive attitude that suggests a balanced, well-rounded person continues to learn more and more about the world, acknowledging the past, enjoying the present, and embracing the challenges of the future. Additionally, this kind of liberal arts education is the natural right of every person.

I reluctantly recall those dead-end days in the seventies when "experts" believed that students should be taught English language and literature that were appropriate to their career interests. Plumbers, say, would not be required to read or write about great literature. I knew this would lead to intellectual slavery and resisted it then and now. UMD, like other institutions, will decentralize, downsize, and restructure again, but its next one hundred years should hold true to the notion that a broad, liberal arts education is the air that gives flight to the heaviest object.

Students lined up to vote in 1964 for UMD's Homecoming queen.

Provost Raymond Darland crowned Sharon Kauppi the 1964 Homecoming Queen at a special ceremony.

109

University of Minnesota policy did not allow a building to be named after anyone presently employed within the University system. Because Provost Darland continued to work part-time in development after his retirement as provost in 1976, no building could be named after him until he permanently retired in 1981. Finally, on June 25, 1982, the new administration building (the last built under Darland) was formally dedicated as the Darland Administration Building.

Restructuring, the most significant reorganization since becoming part of the University of Minnesota in 1947, enabled UMD to function as a genuine university. Restructuring was important but Provost Darland realized that another more difficult step was needed for UMD to reach its potential—greater autonomy within the University of Minnesota system. UMD was being treated as a second-class citizen, he argued, and it needed more autonomy so that it could expand and develop new programs. Darland's efforts in that regard have been continued by his successors. Raymond Darland indeed was a special man—an optimist who was enthusiastic about almost everything he did, especially if it involved UMD. With unbounded energy and profound love, he helped UMD shed its branch campus image and transform itself into a comprehensive university. UMD had come of age.

Groundbreaking ceremonies for the Marshall W. Alworth Planetarium were held on October 13, 1965. Marshall W. Alworth, a prominent Duluth businessman, provided the entire $194,440 funding for the building, which was completed in the spring of 1967. Alworth turned the first spade.

Vice President Hubert H. Humphrey spoke at UMD at commencement ceremonies in the spring of 1966.

Construction began on Griggs Stadium in October 1966. Pictured, left to right, were Bob Murray; Thomas Clure, stadium committee chairman; Roy Teppen; and UMD Athletic Director Lloyd Peterson. Both Murray and Teppen served as presidents of the UMD Alumni Association.

Of the more than 450 athletes who have worn a UMD hockey uniform, perhaps none had more of an impact on the Bulldog program than All-American center Keith "Huffer" Christiansen. On January 30, 1988, Christiansen was paid the ultimate tribute by UMD when his familiar "No. 9" jersey was officially retired. That marked the only time the school had bestowed that honor upon any of its athletes. Christiansen is shown here on November 19, 1966, when he helped christen the new Duluth Arena with a school-record six assists in leading the Bulldogs past the Minnesota Gophers.

Alpha Nu Omega sponsored the 1967 Engagement Ball. The couples received a traditional engagement ring, an engagement certificate, and a corsage. Karen Olson and her partner demonstrated the latest dance moves at the ball.

Left: UMD Provost Darland, left, Senior Student Personnel Worker Connie Jo Skidmore, and UMD Academic Dean Tom Chamberlin celebrated the twentieth anniversary of UMD's affiliation with the University of Minnesota system in July 1967. Skidmore planned and organized the celebration.

Students in 1967 participated in Homecoming fun. One favorite event was "Flush the Johnny."

Right: Provost Darland previewed UMD's first alumni publication, *UMD Alumnotes* (October 1969), with Mary Date, executive secretary of the UMD Alumni Association, and alumnus James Houle.

The reserved style of University of Minnesota President Malcolm Moos, left, and his administrative team contrasted with Provost Darland's exuberance.

Below: During the 1960s and 1970s, northeastern Minnesota was well served by these members of the University of Minnesota Board of Regents: Richard L. Griggs (1939–1963) of Duluth (left), William K. Montague (1963–1968), and Fred Cina (1969–1973) of Aurora.

Above: Harry Reasoner (lower left), CBS News correspondent, delivered the fifth Dalton LeMasurier Lecture in April 1968.

John Ness, speech and communications professor, lectured to a class in 1969. The John Ness award is presented in his memory each spring to a graduating senior in communication with a record of high academic achievement and distinguished service to the university.

A window display in the dorms was a reminder of the "good old days" when alcohol was allowed on campus for those over the drinking age.

Although its roots dated back to the Duluth Normal School era, the women's athletic program at UMD didn't really take off until the arrival of pioneers such as, from left to right, Joann Johnson, Mary Mullin, and Eleanor Rynda, in the late 1960s and early 1970s.

Provost Raymond Darland donned a chef's hat to serve breakfast coffee to students during S.O.S. Week in April 1968.

Sociology Professor Walter Baeumler, left, was remembered by UMD students as someone who taught them the importance of recognizing and solving social problems. In off-hours, he assisted Richard Haney, physical education instructor, with skiing classes. The Walter Baeumler-Mortrud H. Kaplan Holocaust lecture series honors his fervent belief that ignorance about the past leads to bigotry, racism, and violence.

Dr. Kathy Annette, former UMD School of Medicine student, received her M.D. from the University of Minnesota in 1983. Annette did her residency in family medicine in Duluth, before practicing at the Leech Lake and Red Lake reservations. She is now the regional director of the Indian Health Services (IHS), for Minnesota, Wisconsin, Michigan, and Iowa.

UMD students joined a nationwide moratorium on class attendance to protest the Vietnam War on October 15, 1969.

Right: The "Petey Drive" was an annual event sponsored by several sororities on campus. The sororities' goal was to raise money and create awareness of underprivileged people in the community. This particular drive took place in December of 1969.

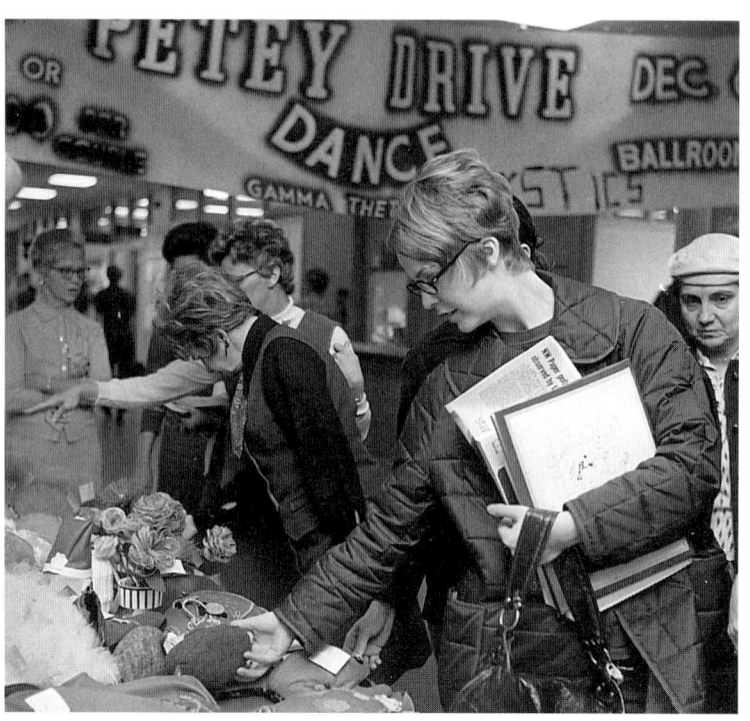

The official groundbreaking ceremonies for the Administration Building were held in December 1969. From left to right were Student Association President Greg Fox, now UMD vice chancellor for the Office of Finance and Operations, Provost Darland, Business Manager Robert Bridges, and Assistant to the Provost Robert Heller.

Below: Students tried to get an old "wreck" rolling again.

121

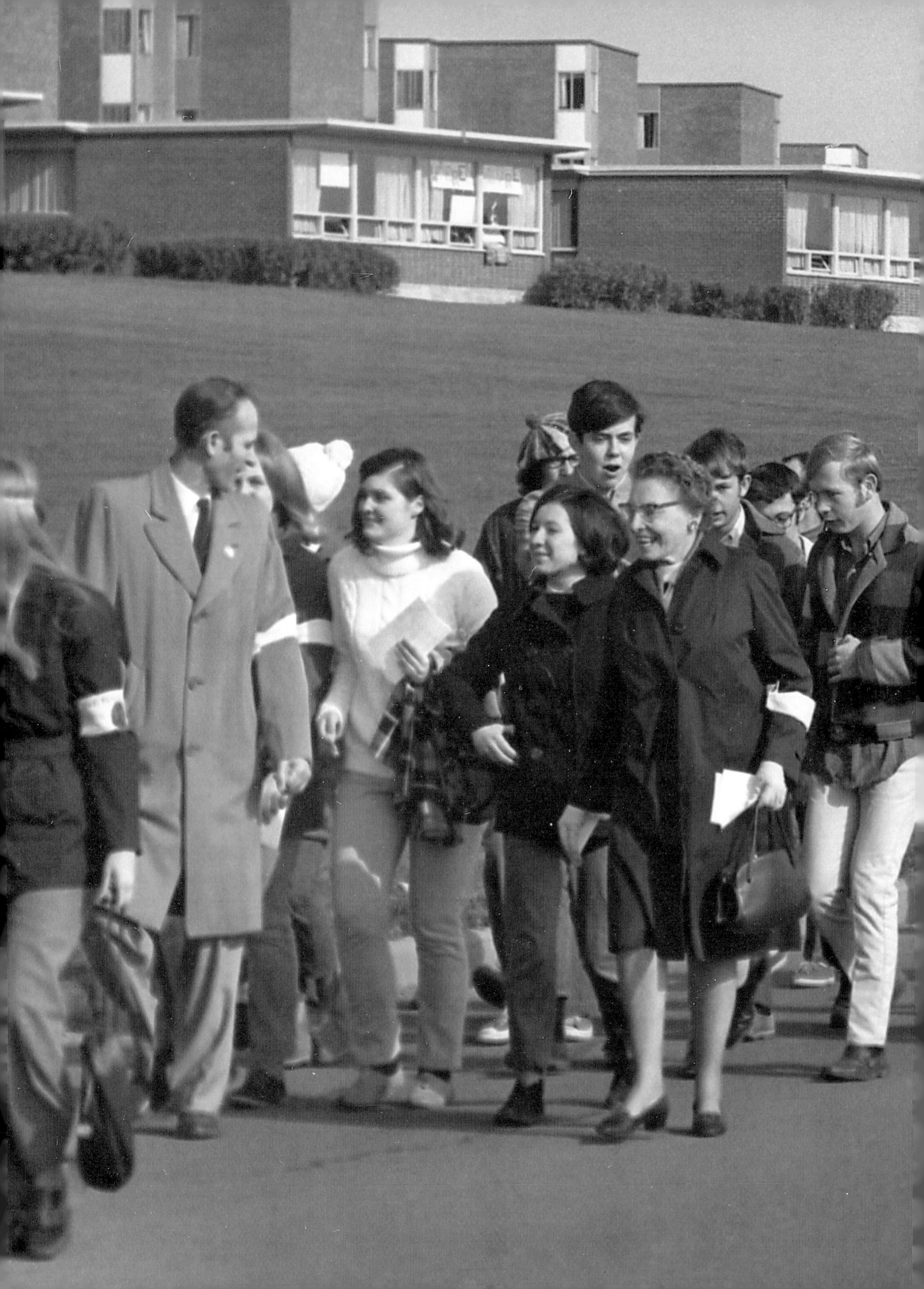

QUESTION:
OVER POPULATION
ANSWER:
WAR.
PESTILENCE.
FAMINE.
BIRTH CONTROL.

The original Movilla units for UMD's Village Apartments, intended as temporary housing when they were erected in 1970, were torn down in 1995. Each apartment accommodated four students. Each unit had two bedrooms, two bathrooms, a living room, and a kitchen.

"Angel Flight" consisted of friends of UMD ROTC cadets. It was primarily a service organization which functioned as a sorority attached to the Air Force ROTC from the early 1960s till the mid-1970s. In 1971 Angel Flight won the national prize as the top Angel Flight unit in the nation. Here, the members displayed their award.

Students boarded the 'intra-campus' bus, which began making cross-campus trips in 1971. Students living in Torrance Hall on the lower campus especially appreciated the service in the winter.

A ROTC cadet had his "wings" clipped after making his first solo flight. ROTC students were commissioned as second lieutenants in the Air Force at commencement ceremonies.

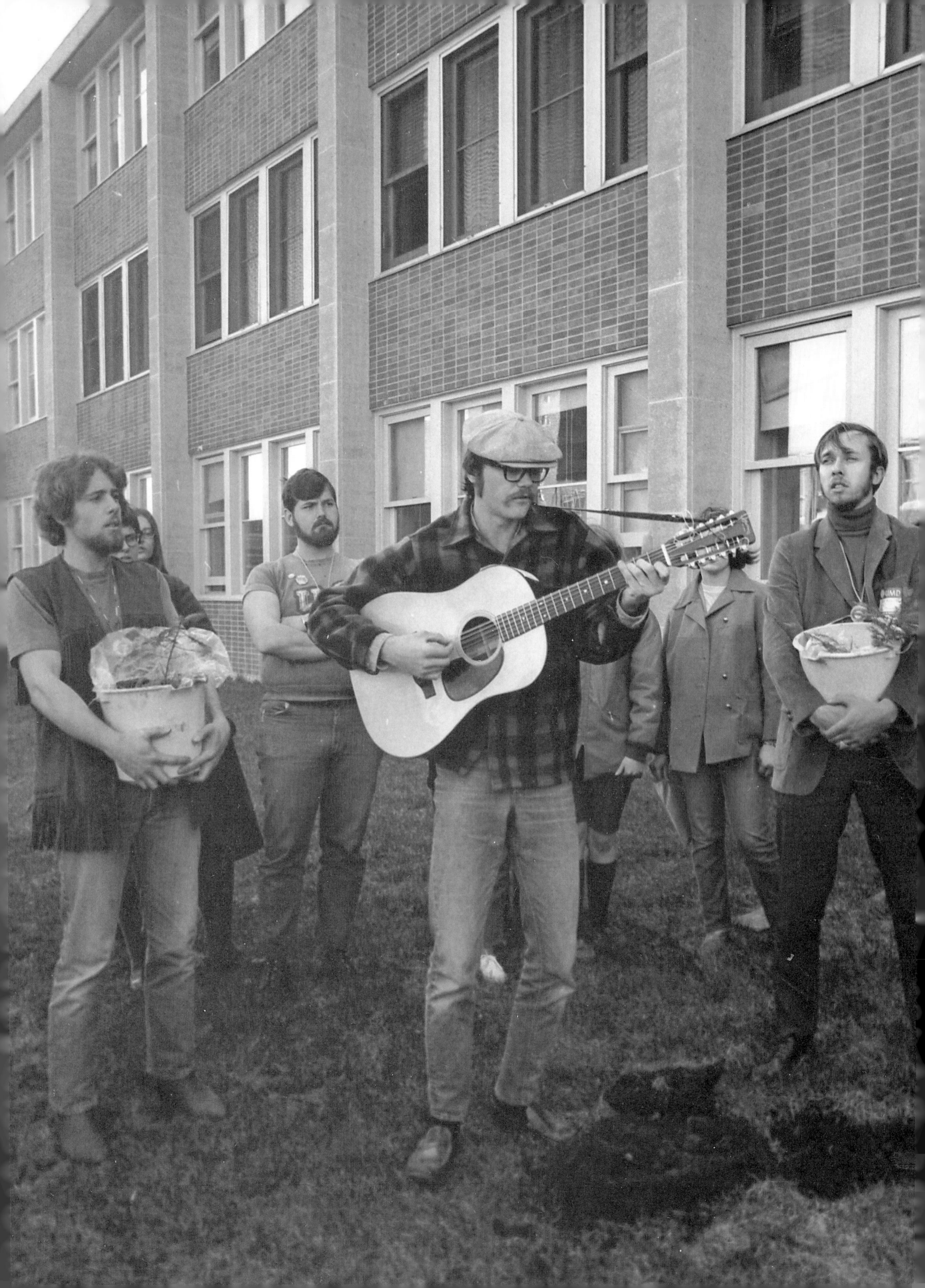

"Oikos," a biology laboratory on wheels, was equipped to help students research Minnesota ecology. Biology Professor Hollie Collins, right, described the bus. The mobile laboratory, nicknamed the "biology bus," operated from 1971 to 1981.

Left: The first "Earth Days" were held on campus in April 1971. The keynote speaker for the three-day event was Stewart Udall, secretary of the Department of the Interior under John F. Kennedy and Lyndon B. Johnson. Several campus groups focused on environmental awareness now participate in the annual event.

Robert E. Powless came to UMD to develop the American Indian Studies program which he has headed since 1988. "I've always felt that helping students is what our job is all about. In all the years I've been here, I have very seldom, if ever, turned a student away from my door who wanted to talk to me," he said. "I would like to think that I gave to the American Indian programs and particularly the Department of American Indian Studies some academic consistency and reliability and respect over the years because of the way that I've operated and the way that I teach my classes.

"I've tried to focus what I do on the students and to make sure that they understand that there are some real advantages in going to college, but that is only a part of their lives and if they are ultimately not successful in it, that doesn't mean they are bad people," Powless added.

William Kunstler, defender of the Chicago Seven, came to UMD as a guest speaker in the spring of 1972. He was introduced by Virginia Katz, professor of speech, communications, and theatre arts, and the 1971–72 chair of the Kirby Lectures and Convocations Committee.

The first class of twenty-four students at the School of Medicine entered in 1972. Pictured in the front row, left to right, were: Dale Bohlke, Betty Bowers, Steve Lucas, Lee Cohen, Maureen Kane, and Barbara Bowers. Second row, left to right: Allan Johns, Edward LaDue Sr., Mary Sue House, Richard Roach, Gary Stelzer, and Toni Magnuson. Third row, left to right: Burton Helleloid, Richard Gustafson, John Wilson, and John Hubert. Fourth row, left to right: Rodney Olson, David Deteret, Michael Clifford, James O'Reilly, Bennett Orvik, Keith Rapp, and Roger Waage.

The popular Elizabethan Dinners began in 1974. The dinners featured food, wandering minstrels, madrigals by the Elizabethan Singers, a court, and jesters. The annual event, led by Professor Vernon Opheim, music, ended in 1987.

Left: A 1973 alumni dinner at Duluth's Kitchi Gammi Club featured Lt. Commander David Wheat, a 1963 UMD graduate who was held prisoner in North Vietnam for seven years. Alumni Association President Gerald Brown welcomed Wheat.

The $2.6 million Marshall Performing Arts Center, named after its generous benefactors, sisters Julia Marshall, Caroline Marshall, and Jessica Marshall Spencer, was formally dedicated on February 3, 1974. The Dudley Experimental Theatre, located within the center, honored the fourth donor, Marjorie Congdon Dudley.

The first UMD production staged in the new Marshall Performing Arts Center was the popular musical, *Hello, Dolly*. Director Roger Schultz offered advice to Kim Wilson, the UMD Theater student who played Dolly. The show sold out its seven-night run.

UMD's Air Force ROTC program began enrolling women in 1971. Bette MacTaggart, left, and Patricia Mankowski were the first female second lieutenants commissioned in UMD's ROTC program. They both graduated in 1975.

In 1978 UMD hosted Soviet chemist Andrei Schegolev, right, shown here with Professor Ron Caple, chemistry. Caple has since collaborated on research projects with several scientists based in the former Soviet Union.

Provost Darland awarded students their diplomas at the spring commencement of 1976, his last as provost of UMD.

UMD REFLECTIONS

Kathryn A. Martin was inaugurated as UMD's eighth chancellor on November 3, 1995.

Right: Maria Casey, left, and Deb Nyquist, UMD medical students, use a video disc player to observe an image of a kidney section.

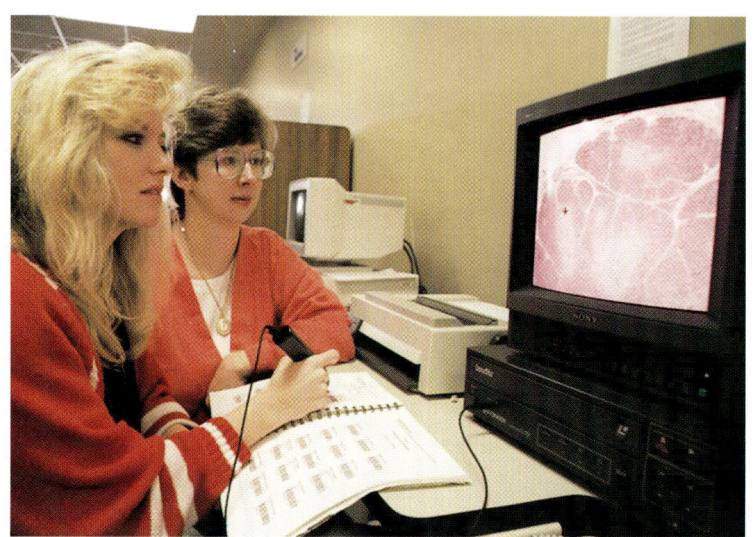

A neon reminder

Left: The new Village Apartments residence halls, completed in the fall of 1995, replaced the Movilla temporary housing units.

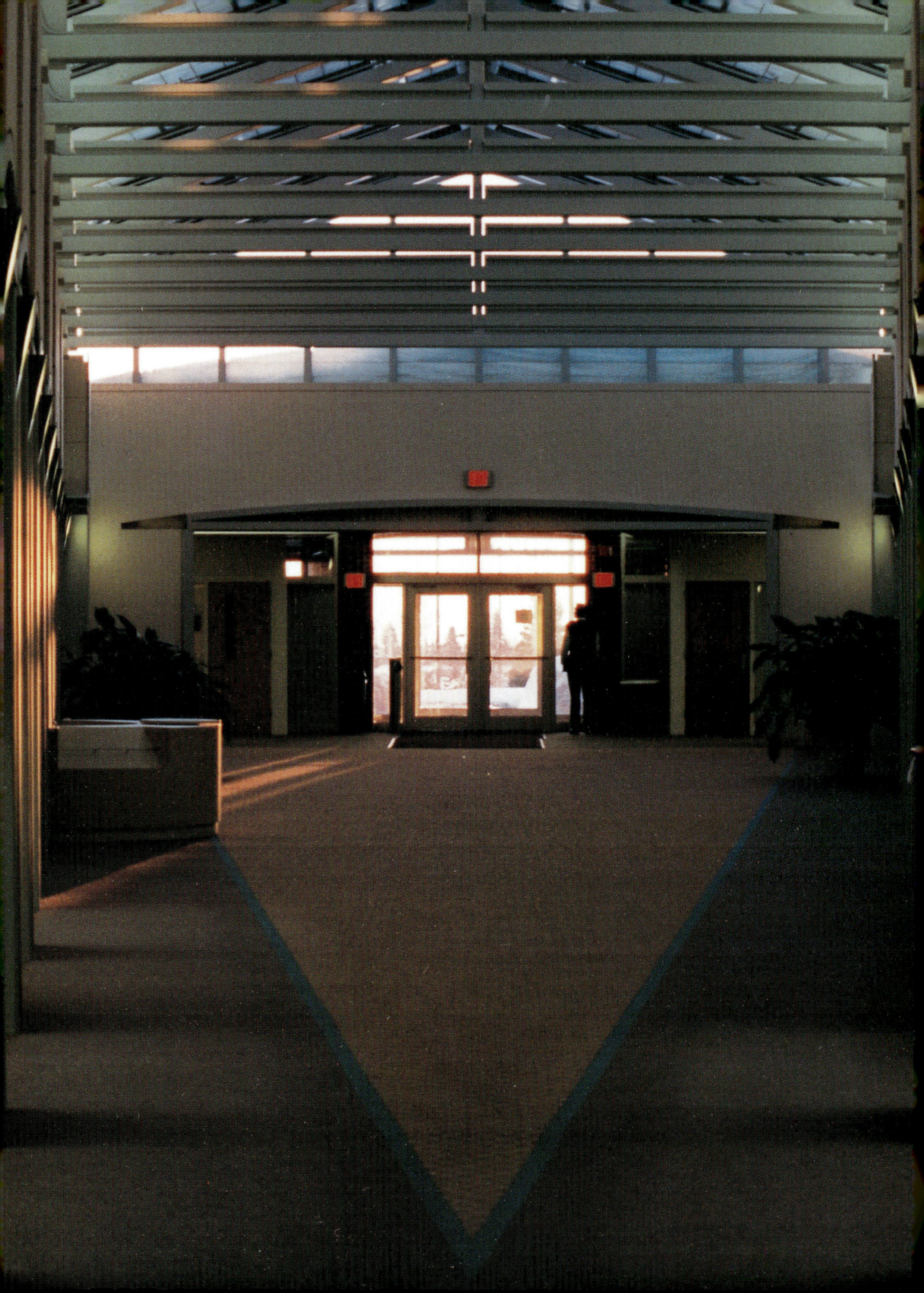

Facing page: On clear days, the Campus Center "Wedge" provides a glimpse of Lake Superior beyond the campus. The triangular space has become a popular UMD gathering spot.

Banners throughout the campus herald UMD's approach to the new partnerships and innovation of the twenty-first century.

Michael Pallansch played Joseph in the 1988 UMD Theatre production of *Joseph and the Amazing Technicolor Dreamcoat*.

Glensheen, a twenty-two-acre historic estate listed on the National Register of Historic Places, was given to the University in 1968 by the heirs of Chester and Clara Congdon. The thirty-nine-room Jacobean revival mansion is flanked by formal gardens and several outbuildings. The estate opened for public tours in 1979.

Anishinabe Days, a celebration of American Indian culture, is held annually at UMD.

Above: Director Martin DeWitt and Jana Pastika, store manager, are pictured in the Tweed Museum of Art. Considered one of northeastern Minnesota's most important cultural resources, the museum collection now includes more than thirty-five hundred sculptures, paintings, drawings, and other fine art objects.

Left: A physics student conducts an experiment in the laser lab.

Below left: Students enrolled in UMD's graduate programs can choose from seventeen different fields. Here a chemistry M.S. student works in one of several campus laboratories.

Above: In 1989–90, UMD All-Americans Dina Kangas, basketball, Chad Erickson, hockey, and Jay Guidinger, basketball, grabbed state and national headlines for their sportsmanship and athletic skills.

Left: The UMD School of Medicine provides state-of-the-art training facilities for its medical students.

The Marshall Performing Arts Center is an important UMD and community cultural resource.

Two greenhouses are connected to the UMD Life Sciences Building.

The expansion of the UMD campus can best be captured from the air.

Ordean Court is the courtyard entrance to the east campus buildings and the Marshall Performing Arts Center, In 1965, Ordean provided funds to commission the statue of Daniel Greysolon, Sieur du Lhut, by sculptor Jacques Lipchitz.

Right: On the edge of Lake Superior, and on the cutting edge of Great Lakes research, faculty at UMD's Large Lakes Observatory are discovering new facts about lake environments.

SOCRATES
MONROVIA

The atrium in the School of Business and Economics provides a welcoming environment for students.

UMD students canoe on Rock Pond in the William R. Bagley Nature Area, a thirteen-acre woodland given to the university in 1953 by the William R. Bagley family.

The campus entrance sign greets UMD visitors.

Dale Baker, right, associate director, and Mike McDonald, director, conducted research in Lake Superior for the Minnesota Sea Grant Extension Program. Housed at UMD, Sea Grant provides several research opportunities for UMD undergraduate and graduate students.

ROBERT HELLER: THE GROWING MATURITY OF UMD

1976–1987

CHAPTER FIVE

Robert Heller served UMD as acting provost, provost, and chancellor (the title "chancellor" replaced that of "provost" in 1985) from 1976 to 1987, an era marked by the development of valuable programs. Members of the UMD community still remember Heller's friendly, low-key leadership style, hard work, and above all, his complete dedication to UMD—he was everywhere doing everything. Bob Heller loved UMD!

Heller knew the faculty, community, and the political realities of UMD's situation. Hired to teach geology in 1950, he built the department and never lost interest in it. Indeed, geology remained a lifelong passion; he was always studying and commenting on geological formations. While retaining a lively interest in research, he devoted much of his career to administration, serving as head of the Department of Geology, assistant to the provost, assistant provost, acting provost, provost, and chancellor. His interest in creating new programs was one of his many strengths. Given his passion for new programs, it is not surprising that the chancellor frequently found himself in difficult situations. Heller pushed for rapid expansion of the Duluth campus, but he had to contend with the president of the University of Minnesota and other central administrators in Minneapolis who envisioned a far more modest role for UMD. The chancellor's drive for new programs

University of Minnesota Regent Erwin L. Goldfine (1975–1987) of Duluth, far left, joined Provost Emeritus Raymond Darland; Clarence Anderson, formerly UMD's University Relations representative; and Acting Provost Robert Heller in the processional line-up for the 1976 summer commencement, the last summer graduation ceremony held at UMD.

was based on his vision for the campus. UMD was to be a comprehensive university offering liberal arts, graduate, and professional programs. To realize this vision, Heller needed a talented faculty, interested in both teaching and research, and state-of-the-art physical facilities. Facing stiff opposition from Minneapolis, the chancellor had to rely on area legislators to fight for the growth and development of the Duluth campus. Despite serious differences with central administration and severe financial limitations, Heller established valuable programs that helped to fulfill his dreams of an important university.

Right: In September 1980, thanks to the efforts of many people, three faculty members and fifty students initiated the first year-long study abroad program in the University of Minnesota system. Students in the first group posed outside the University of Birmingham's library in England. From left to right are, Macy Dickson, Nancy Michoy, Sue Ellis, Pattie Leslie, Eric Hylden, Betsy Alamisa, Mary McGintey, Sue Ann Renslen, and John Miller.

LIBRARY

Students sharing a desk in Griggs found inspiration in Uncle Sam and a student in a Burntside room surrounded herself with photos and other memorabilia.

Heller's interest in creating a study-abroad program began in 1968 when he participated in an international education symposium in Varna, Bulgaria. The conference convinced him that UMD should offer its students the rich educational opportunities of studying abroad. His own time in Europe and his daughter's positive experience with a study-abroad program strengthened his resolve. With characteristic enthusiasm he worked to create similar opportunities for UMD students. Pressure from other projects, such as the medical school, delayed initiation; but in February 1978, a task force chaired by Valworth R. Plumb concluded that study abroad would be an asset for UMD. The next step, and it proved formidable, was to find a British university with space to house the program. After negotiating with a number of universities, UMD found its partner, the University of Birmingham.

James Grant, a UMD geology professor, and his wife Christabel were particularly intrigued by the study-abroad concept. They interested Eunice Phillips, Christabel's sister, in UMD's ideas. Phillips, who was principal of the Rugby Girls High School in Rugby, England, secured the assistance of John

Head Coach Mike Sertich and the Bulldogs had plenty of reasons to celebrate on the night of February 17, 1984, when UMD claimed its first Western Collegiate Hockey Association (WCHA) championship with a 4-2 win over the University of Wisconsin. Sertich, who also directed the Bulldogs to league titles in 1985 and 1993, was the first individual to be named the WCHA's Coach of the Year on three straight occasions (1983–85) and the second to win the award four or more times (1983–85 and 1993).

149

George "Rip" Rapp Jr., geoarchaeology, arrived at UMD in 1975. He is presently director of the Archaeometry Laboratory and was named UMD's first Regents' Professor in 1995, one of only twenty in the University system. He also is the first Regents' Professor from an outstate campus. Rapp was the first dean of the College of Letters and Science and the founding dean of the College of Science and Engineering. He played important roles in the development of the engineering programs and graduate programs in computer science, in advocating personal computer availability for students on campus, in the development of the Northeast Minnesota Historical Center, in the Master of Liberal Studies degree, and in the Archaeometry Laboratory. A veteran of countless archaeological expeditions, Rapp challenged the popular historical conception that the chariot battles in Homer's *Iliad* took place on a broad plain outside of Troy. "We went out there...drilled holes...studied the sequence of geological environments and showed that at the time of the Trojan War, the plain was under water, so the chariots would have to have had pontoons," he said.

A student found a quiet study space in the Tweed Museum of Art.

Fathers, the finance and operations officer of the University of Birmingham. Fathers, a warm, friendly man with the ability to get things done, was the essential champion of UMD's proposal to Birmingham's administration and continued to be the program's mentor and advocate until his retirement.

On January 9, 1980, a committee was appointed to plan the curriculum for UMD's first study-abroad program. Heller was pleased with the results. Chaired by Jonathan Conant, a professor of German, the committee included Wendell Glick, James Grant, Roy Hoover, Klaus Jankofsky, M. Harry Lease, Raymond Raab, Jean Swanson, Albert Tezla, Bruce Goode, Howard Meyer, and Renae Rogers. In September 1980, thanks to the efforts of many, UMD initiated the first year-long study abroad program in the University of Minnesota system.

The Study in England Program, now housed at the University of Central England in Birmingham, continues to offer a full academic year of study to about fifty undergraduates a year. In addition, UMD provides opportunities to study and travel in Sweden, Finland, and France.

Chancellor Heller considered the creation and development of UMD's Study Abroad Program to be one of the most satisfying aspects of his career. He saw the program as a valuable asset for the faculty as well as the students. Study Abroad owes its origins to Heller's commitment and determination, remaining an enduring reminder of his legacy to UMD.

The Royal D. Alworth Jr. Institute for International Studies, established in 1987, brings thought-provoking speakers to campus. One example will have to suffice. The Institute sponsored a 1994 lecture on the Middle East by Pulitzer Prize-winning author and frequent television commentator, Thomas Friedman of the *New York Times*. Interest in international issues is also fostered by Alworth-sponsored lectures and lunchtime "brown bag" presentations. UMD faculty, including visiting faculty from abroad, discuss politics and diplomacy and the scientific, cultural, and artistic contributions of particular countries and regions.

With the help of Judge Gerald W. Heaney, Chancellor Heller also played a key role in fulfilling a longstanding goal of northeastern Minnesota—the establishment of a natural resources institute at UMD. An institute was needed to conduct research on minerals, alternative energy, forest products, and water. Many friends of UMD argued that research on minerals and forest products should be done in their natural environments. UMD was the logical site. Efforts to move the University's Minneapolis-based School of Mines to UMD in the early to mid-1950s had been prevented by a lack of technical departments on the Duluth campus and by opposition from the

UMD Theatre's production of *Homesteaders* played to standing-room-only crowds in 1987 at the national American College Theatre Festival (ACTF) at the Kennedy Center for the Performing Arts in Washington, D.C. *Homesteaders* was selected one of the five best college theatre productions in the country by ACTF jurors—the highest honor for a collegiate theatre program. The production was directed by Harvey Jordan, far right, and written by Nina Schengold, far right front. The cast included, from the left, Patty Hall, Tim McGee, Sally Nysteun, Brett Rickaby, and Colleen Heffernan.

Below: During sixty-plus seasons of intercollegiate football, UMD has produced a legion of standout running backs, but no Bulldog carried the football more efficiently than Ted McKnight. McKnight, named a 1976 Associated Press All-American, finished his college career with the highest rushing yardage total in UMD history. He then played NFL football for six years with the Kansas City Chiefs and the Buffalo Bills.

The Council of Religious Advisors has proved important in the lives of many UMD students. Father George Schroeder, center, talked with students. Today, ten campus ministries serve UMD.

The UMD International Club has sponsored "The Feast of Nations," an annual event which benefits the organization, since 1966. Above, foreign and American students sampled various foreign cuisines.

Richard Ojakangas joined UMD's Department of Geology in 1964. "When I was an undergraduate back in the 1950s, a young professor by the name of Bob Heller talked me into switching from business/economics to geology. It is a decision that I have never regretted, even for one moment," he said. "And finally ending up back here at UMD, teaching and conducting research in an excellent department with eager students and stimulating colleagues, amid an excellent and growing university, has made the past thirty-one years most rewarding and enjoyable. Also, our three children and my wife Beatrice have all graduated from UMD, so UMD is a family affair!"

Governor Rudy Perpich, right, congratulated Natural Resources Research Institute (NRRI) Director Mike Lalich at the 1986 dedication of the NRRI building, the former site of the U.S. Air Force base in Duluth. NRRI opened after extensive efforts from the Governor's office, UMD administrators, and Minnesota legislative, industry, and community leaders.

Twin Cities campus. Despite the problems, State Representative Francis (Frenchy) La Brosse did propose that the schools of Mines and Forestry be moved to UMD. This attempt and other similar efforts failed, but the friends of UMD kept the idea of a resource institute alive.

Devastating conditions in the taconite industry, backbone of northeastern Minnesota's economy, motivated business and political leaders in the early 1980s to fight for a research center at UMD that would help to diversify the region's economy. Chancellor Heller found himself in a most difficult and disagreeable situation when University President C. Peter Magrath ordered him not to lobby for a research institute at UMD. Fortunately, Governor Rudy Perpich, a native of northeastern Minnesota, appointed a committee to determine the feasibility of the concept. Judge Heaney, a member of the committee, worked to gain political support throughout the state. Heller, in a behind-the-scenes effort, worked closely with Heaney. The 1983 establishment of the Natural Resources Research Institute (NRRI) was truly the work of many—too many to name—but the work of Judge Heaney was the *sine qua non* of success.

UMD faculty were quick to seize the opportunities that NRRI provided. Ralph W. Marsden, professor emeritus of the Department of Geology, helped to conceptualize the Institute and its mission. This volunteer, remembered for his enthusiasm, integrity, and foresight, structured many of the programs that have made NRRI such a valuable resource. NRRI, first housed on

UMD's lower campus, was headed by acting coordinator Jerrold Peterson, a professor of economics. The Institute has become a valuable element in UMD's teaching and research mission.

Under the leadership of Michael Lalich, who became director on March 1, 1984, NRRI has developed into a major resource that serves the entire state. Now located on the former Duluth Air Force Base in the Semi-Automatic Ground Environment Building, NRRI has a staff of more than two hundred scientists, engineers, business experts, and students who conduct research that fosters private sector employment.

In addition to fostering employment and protecting the environment, NRRI has fulfilled Chancellor Heller's academic goals: UMD faculty and students conduct research at the Institute, and several NRRI employees hold faculty or adjunct faculty positions. NRRI assists students by providing scholarships and research assistantships, including some designed to interest minorities in science careers. Moreover, the applied research skills learned at NRRI are invaluable in securing employment after graduation. NRRI's outreach mission provides an excellent model for growth and development. If UMD is to prosper, it must be recognized as a comprehensive educational, cultural, and research center that serves all of Minnesota and beyond.

The Minnesota Repertory Theatre's 1976 grand opening was celebrated with balloons and an Ordean Court party. The Rep was a summer theatre group made up of UMD faculty, students, and visiting artists. The Rep troupe staged three to four productions per season, ranging from Shakespeare to Broadway musicals to modern drama. The group was forced to end its seventeen-year run in 1993 due to University system-wide budget cuts.

UMD's Health Science Library addition opened in 1978. It has become the major medical library resource in the region.

The fall 1978 UMD Theatre production of *Cinderella* appealed to young theatre enthusiasts.

Glenn Nelson, professor emeritus of art, is an internationally acclaimed ceramist. He retired from UMD in 1975. Students of Glenn Nelson will always remember this highly talented and influential ceramics professor. The Tweed Museum of Art is home to many of Nelson's works, in addition to those he collected from around the world.

Above Right: The UMD School of Medicine's current complex was built during 1977–78. It was occupied on February 19, 1979, and officially dedicated on September 15, 1979.

In 1979 the combined estates of Jonathan, Simon, and Milton Sax were bequeathed to the Tweed Museum of Art. The gift established the Sax Purchase Fund for acquisitions to the Tweed permanent collection and financed construction of the Sax Gallery. Pictured at the signing are (from left to right): Ray Darland, provost emeritus; William Boyce, director, Tweed Art Museum; Laverne Sax; Adrienne Josephs; and Phillip Coffman, dean, School of Fine Arts. Accumulated interest from the Sax endowment constructed the Sax Sculpture Conservatory (four hundred square feet of exhibition space) and has continued to develop the Tweed acquisition program.

The Home Economics Building was renamed Montague Hall in honor of William K. Montague at a dedication on October 4, 1982. Montague served as a University of Minnesota Regent from 1963 to 1969. An attorney, an assistant attorney general of Minnesota, and a longtime Shakespeare buff, Montague was also known as the author of *The Man of Stratford—The Real Shakespeare*, a refutation of claims that Bacon and others wrote Shakespeare's works.

James Shearer, who graduated from UMD in 1969, has drawn on his own undergraduate experiences as an advocate for students with disabilities. Shearer served as coordinator of handicapped student services from 1973 to 1979 and is presently associate director of the UMD facilities management department. "UMD took an early leadership position in being able to offer students with disabilities equal access to higher education in Minnesota," Shearer said. "Both the architectural planning of the facilities and the programmatic support offered have been a real tradition here."

Don Pearce, who retired as UMD Library director in 1988, was instrumental in documenting the Ramseyer-Northern Bible Society Museum Collection, which was given to UMD in 1979. The collection, which includes most of the major four Torahs from the fifteenth to nineteenth centuries, was started by Henry Ramseyer and was maintained by the Northern Bible Society after his death in the 1940s.

Four-year degree programs in computer engineering, industrial engineering, and chemical engineering were developed in the 1980s. The first eleven chemical engineering graduates received their B.S. degrees in 1987. Presently, 25 percent of all UMD chemical engineering students are female. Above, Brian Whipps and Dionne Nelson experimented with heat transfer.

The economic plight of northeastern Minnesota also provided a powerful incentive to establish engineering programs at UMD. Chancellor Heller, Dean of the College of Letters and Science George "Rip" Rapp, and countless other administrators and faculty saw and seized that opportunity. They faced an uphill struggle that required the efforts of civic and political leaders such as Governor Perpich, Mayor John Fedo of Duluth, Judge Heaney, Regent Goldfine, and legislators from the northeastern districts. Business leaders such as Jack F. Rowe, John F. Johnson, and Robert J. Marchetti, all representing Minnesota Power, played key roles. Support from the political and business communities was so great that it overcame opposition from President Magrath. In 1983 the state legislature authorized UMD programs in chemical engineering, electrical and computer engineering, and industrial engineering.

Minnesota Power continued its generous role in 1986 by establishing the Jack Rowe Minnesota Power Chair in Electrical and Computer Engineering, the first endowed faculty chair at UMD. This endowed professorship gave UMD the important hallmark of an older and larger research university.

UMD was particularly well-represented in the 1980 Winter Olympics Games in Lake Placid, New York. Jim Denney, left, John Harrington, and Mark Pavelich displayed their gold medals. Denney had won a bronze medal in ski jumping in 1976.

Jerrold Peterson, professor of economics (left), and Glenn Gronseth, economics research associate, jointly produced the Duluth Business Index in 1982 and 1983. Gronseth, employed by the Minnesota Job Service before coming to UMD in 1982, co-founded the Index in 1964 with Cecil Meyer, an economics professor at UMD. Peterson was named the acting coordinator of NRRI in 1983.

Erwin Goldfine, a Duluth businessman, served as a University of Minnesota Regent from 1975 to 1987. He continues to support UMD's development efforts. "Serving as a regent of the University of Minnesota was the highlight of my life," he said. "The over twelve years I was associated with the University were wonderful years for my wife and me. I would get up at five in the morning, and I dedicated the first three hours of every day to University business . . . for every minute I put in I got fifteen minutes' reward."

Jane Maddy joined UMD's Department of Psychology in 1967. She was one of the early pioneers in making Women's Studies a recognized departmental discipline and served as head of UMD's Commission on Women from 1979 to 1981. "There weren't many women faculty when I came," she said. "Over the years, it has been one of my UMD blessings to see more bright and capable women entering academia and choosing this campus on which to build their careers."

Head Coach Mike Sertich, left, and senior Bulldogs defenseman Tom Kurvers were all smiles following Kurvers' selection as the winner of the 1983–84 Hobey Baker Memorial Award, given to the outstanding collegiate hockey player in the United States. One year later, winger Bill Watson received the award, and another Bulldog winger, Chris Marinucci, received the award in 1994. At the time Marinucci received the award, only Harvard University boasted three winners of the prestigious honor.

Students enjoyed wearing their robes and caps for the first time on Cap and Gown Day, a tradition which no longer exists.

In the decade since, UMD has added five more endowed chairs and two visiting professorships. These include the Royal D. Alworth Jr. Professorship in Northern Circle Studies, the Robert L. Heller Professorship in Geology, the Margaret Mitchell Curator of the Tweed Museum, the Ruth Myers Professorship in American Indian Education, the Edwin Eddy Professorship in Neurocommunication Disorders at the School of Medicine, the 3M William L. Knight Distinguished Visiting Professorship in Technology Development, and the Visiting Professorship in Finance and Management.

In addition to its increasingly important role in Minnesota's economy, especially in the northeastern region, UMD has made important strides in meeting human service needs. In May 1972, the University of Minnesota Board of Regents approved a Master of Social Work degree for UMD. The new UMD School of Social Development opened in August with a class of twenty-three students. Under the leadership of the school's first director, John F. Jones, the M.S.W. program focused on social development and planned social change.

Faced with budget constraints in the mid-1980s, the School of Social Development became a department in the newly formed College of Education and Human Service Professions. The graduate program in social work was eliminated. Fortunately, a new M.S.W. program was created in 1987. This program was designed to prepare students for direct services, administration, and community development. Social work has since emerged as UMD's largest graduate program in terms of total numbers and numbers of minority students enrolled. Dennis Falk, the Director of Graduate Students for the M.S.W. program, reports that "a continuing emphasis in social work programs at UMD has been efforts to work with American Indian communities to meet their needs. A close connection with American Indian communities has been forged, beginning in the 1970s, by actively recruiting American Indian students, holding conferences on reservations, having Indian speakers on campus, and providing student internships on reservations." In 1995 two of seven faculty members were American Indians. More than twenty American Indian students have received Social Work degrees at UMD.

Another important step in diversifying UMD occurred in 1981 when the Board of Regents approved the creation of a minor in women's studies. The Women's Coordinating Committee worked more than half a decade to create an interdisciplinary program designed to build an awareness of the cultural and historical experiences of women. Among the pioneers in the field at UMD were Jane E. Maddy, psychology; Edith J. Hols, English; Judith A. Trolander, history; Bilin P. Tsai, chemistry; and Mary Zimmerman, behavioral sciences, School of Medicine. Susan Coultrap-McQuin, hired to head the program, proved to be an outstanding teacher, scholar, and administrator. By the end of the program's first year, ten courses in women's studies were offered by faculty in various departments. Six years later the number of courses had grown to forty across campus. This impressive growth enabled women's studies to become a department in its own right. The Department of Women's Studies offers both a major and a minor.

Women's Studies regards community outreach as an important mission of its program. The department sponsors presentations of faculty research, coordinates Women's History Month, publishes a monthly newsletter, and produces a highly regarded collection of student honors papers each year.

Chancellor Heller wanted to see UMD grow and reach its potential as an integral part of the University of Minnesota. He opposed and helped defeat proposals for complete autonomy in the 1980s. He feared that an independent campus in northeastern Minnesota would not thrive once Governor Perpich was out of office. Moreover, he realized that reapportionment had left northeastern Minnesota with a rather narrow base in the legislature. In addition to political considerations, the chancellor argued that being part of the University of Minnesota attracted outstanding faculty and students. Given his pride in UMD, it is not surprising that Heller

Ann Anderson, a 1957 UMD graduate, joined the Department of Music at UMD in 1968. The violinist is also the associate concertmaster of the Duluth-Superior Symphony Orchestra (DSSO). "As a music major in the UMD music department and now as a full professor here, I have benefited immeasurably from the university's association with the DSSO," she said. "The DSSO has provided professional orchestral training and employment for my many students who now take leadership roles in the symphony and who also are teaching in the Duluth area school systems." Ann Anderson, former president of the UMD Alumni Association, established an endowed scholarship in the Master of Liberal Studies program.

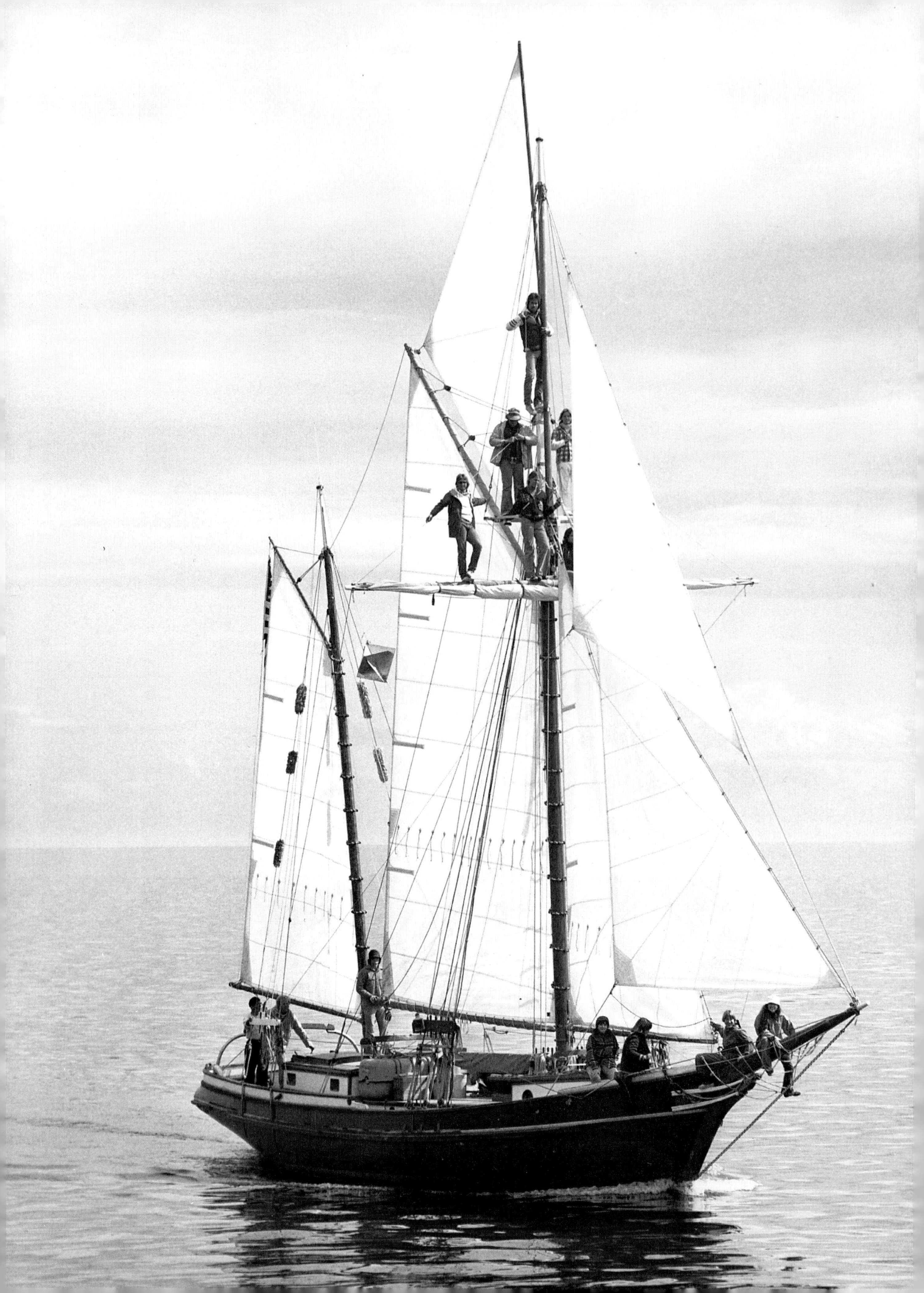

Denise R. Pederson, '84, broke a thirty-seven year record of male leadership in student government at UMD when she was elected president of the Student Association (SA) in 1983. Through the years, SA has represented the students in issues such as tuition increases, faculty evaluations, activity fees, liquor use on campus, racial discrimination, athletic disparities, and restroom facilities.

Hockey fans showed their "Bulldog spirit."

Left: A Freshman Camp crew experiences the thrill of sailing on Lake Superior on a Bayfield-to-Duluth run in the early 1970s.

Gian Carlo Menotti, left, regarded as one of the greatest living composers of opera, visited UMD for a four-day residency in February 1984.

favored greater autonomy for the Duluth campus and was determined to see UMD treated like a coordinate and not a subordinate campus.

Many faculty members shared Chancellor Heller's perception of the need for greater autonomy. Indeed, concerns about the policies of central administration in Minneapolis helped fuel the campaign to unionize the Duluth campus. In May 1980 UMD faculty members voted by a wide margin for union representation. There were three choices on the ballot—no agent, the American Association of University Professors (AAUP), and the UMD Education Association (UMDEA), an affiliate of the National Education Association and the Minnesota Education Association. A runoff election was needed between the two top vote recipients—the AAUP and UMDEA—since none of the groups had received a majority of the total votes cast.

The debate over unionization revealed a wide range of faculty attitudes toward governance. Many who opposed the effort to unionize the campus felt that UMD did not need a union. They argued that a union was unprofessional and had no place in higher education. The supporters of unionization pointed to the dramatic decline in purchasing power suffered by the faculty. Their cause was greatly abetted by discontent over the way salary increases were distributed. The drive for a union was also strengthened by concerns over tenure, promotion, grievance procedures, and job security. The leaders of the AAUP campaign, Dean Crawford, Roger Fischer, Wendell Glick, Craig Grau, and Eleanor Hoffman, forged a campaign in accordance with their beliefs, values, and ideals. AAUP, with its impressive record of defending higher education faculty and academic freedom, appealed to many who regarded it as a more professional organization. The UMDEA leaders, Thomas Bacig, Thomas Boman, A. Dean Hendrickson, and James Nelson, maintained that AAUP lacked the financial and legal resources to be effective. Many faculty members who supported UMDEA thought that AAUP was a novice in collective bargaining and too

The Native Americans into Medicine (NAM) program began in 1984. The program emphasizes identifying, supporting, educating, facilitating entry, and retaining American Indian students in the health sciences, with a major concentration in careers in medicine. Donald Murdock, NAM coordinator, advised students. More than 10 percent of Native American medical students in the United States graduate from the University of Minnesota.

The Walter Mondale/Geraldine Ferraro campaign came to UMD when Mondale addressed an overflow crowd on October 30, 1984. This was Mondale's final campaign stop in Minnesota before the election, which he lost to Ronald Reagan.

much of a "gentlemen's" organization to successfully engage in the rough-and-tumble of negotiations.

UMDEA launched a vigorous campaign. As a result of the October runoff election, it became the first faculty bargaining agent on the Duluth campus. UMDEA received 155, or 57 percent of the ballots cast; AAUP received 118, or 43 percent. In late January 1981, faculty members at the University of Minnesota Waseca voted in favor of collective bargaining and joined forces with their colleagues at UMD in what became known as the University Education Association (UEA).

Many former no-agent and AAUP supporters joined UEA, becoming active in the protracted negotiations that finally led to the first contract ratified by the Board of Regents in January 1983. Richard Lichty, UEA president, and Thomas Bacig, chief negotiator, reported that much of UEA's success in negotiations was made possible by political help from Governor Rudy Perpich and legislators from northern Minnesota. In addition to standardizing procedures and protecting faculty rights, UEA became an important advocate for UMD. Union officials have continued to play a vital role in governance and have supported greater autonomy for the Duluth campus.

While UMD faculty considered unionization, another University of Minnesota faculty issue received substantial press coverage when the University and Shyamala Rajender, a temporary professor in the Department of Chemistry on the Twin Cities campus, signed the Rajender Consent Decree in 1980. The result of Rajender's sex discrimination lawsuit against the

Joe DeLisle, left, and Jim Johnson, received some between-period refreshments during UMD's "hockey first"—a game against a Soviet team and a tour of the Soviet Union—in December 1984.

Left: Moscow State University Pro Rector Uri Tropin, right, lifted his glasses to get a better look at the silver UMD cup presented to him by Provost Heller, who accompanied the Bulldogs hockey team to the Soviet Union.

Students thronged Kirby Student Center during the break between classes.

University, the decree forced the University to change its hiring, promotion, and tenure practices to be more inclusive. An immediate financial and operational consequence for the University was that prospective and present women faculty members were able to file claims against the University if they believed they had been discriminated against. While the numerous claims at the Twin Cities campus tended to be the most visible, several claims were also filed at UMD. Despite the controversial lawsuits and settlements of claims associated with it, the Rajender Decree has led to more equitable representation of women in administrative positions and in departments, particularly in disciplines where women historically have been underrepresented.

The politically charged atmosphere of the early 1980s did not lessen Heller's pride in UMD. Thrilled by Bulldog successes in hockey, Heller, an avid fan, was quick to praise the character of the players both on and off the ice. The chancellor highlighted the talent, hard work, and commitment of the players, the coaches, and staff, especially head coach Mike Sertich, who guided the team to a WCHA championship in 1984. Heller continually reminded fans that the success of UMD athletics would not have been possible without the dreams and hard work of the late athletic director, Ralph Romano.

UMD's contributions to the arts were another source of pride. Heller's last year as chancellor was brightened by UMD's success in the American College Theatre Festival, in which over six hundred colleges and universities from across the country competed. In May 1987 Heller informed the Board of Regents that UMD's play *Homesteaders* was judged best in the region and that the students and staff had won top honors for acting, sets, and costumes.

Directed by Harvey Jordan, *Homesteaders* was judged to be one of the top college and university plays of the season. The cast was invited to Washington, D.C., to perform at the Kennedy Center. Chancellor Heller and his wife Gerry attended two Washington performances that drew capacity crowds and received standing ovations.

Describing facilities and programs to the Board of Regents, Heller stressed that UMD had "one of the best university art museums in the country" and would soon have an even better one when the Sax Sculpture Conservatory was added in 1988. The chancellor also spoke with pride about the contributions made by NRRI, the engineering departments, and the School of Medicine. Heller highlighted the quality of the faculty and students, noting that UMD received more research money than any other college or university in Minnesota except for the Twin Cities campus. Citing the quality of research done at UMD,

UMD honored Chancellor Emeritus Robert L. Heller on September 30, 1988, by renaming the Mathematics-Geology Building Heller Hall. Unveiling the new building sign at the dedication ceremony were Heller, left, his wife, Gerry Heller, and Chancellor Lawrence Ianni.

Marsha Bevard Kulick received her B.A. in therapeutic recreation in 1984 and her M.A. in health education in 1988. She was a record-setting wheelchair athlete who counted among her many awards and honors seven gold medals at the International Wheelchair Olympic Games in 1981; six gold medals in swimming at the Olympic Games for the Disabled in 1984; and numerous world records in disabled swimming events. She was selected as one of ten Outstanding Young Women of America in 1985 and won the Healthy American Fitness Leader Award by the President's Council on Physical Fitness and Sports, the first disabled recipient of that award.

Kay Slack, volunteer chair for the UMD Fund capital campaign, presented a special chair in 1986 to Jack Rowe for the Jack Rowe Chair in Engineering. Minnesota Power donated this first endowed faculty chair to honor Rowe, who had recently retired as the company's chief executive officer.

Heller informed the Regents that UMD had "many of the characteristics of larger, older universities" but still stressed undergraduate education as its primary mission. On September 30, 1988, a grateful UMD honored Chancellor Emeritus Heller by renaming the Mathematics-Geology building Heller Hall. This well-deserved honor recognized his long-standing commitment to UMD and his outstanding achievements.

Professors Charles Matsch, featured, and Richard Ojakangas, geology, established Camp UMD in the Northern Sentinel Range of the Ellsworth Mountains in West Antarctica while participating in an international expedition in 1979–80. As a result of their research, Matsch Ridge and Mount Ojakangas were named in their honor.

Left: Pilot flotation studies on removal of waste materials from iron ore were conducted at NRRI's Coleraine Minerals Research Laboratory. The research was one of many projects which have helped Minnesota's taconite industry remain globally competitive.

More than two hundred graduates from the years 1920 to 1948, former students, and friends attended the 1986 summer reunion for the Duluth State Teachers College. The graduates gathered on the familiar steps of Old Main.

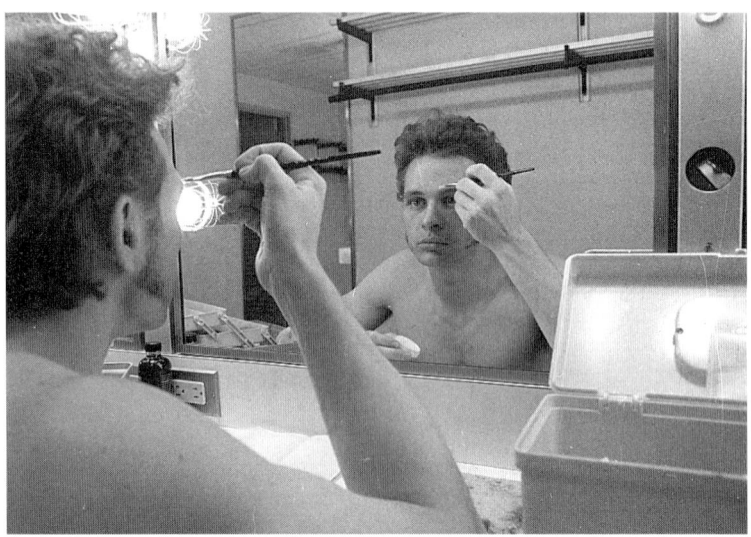

In 1987, UMD Theatre student Brett Rickaby was selected as one of two national winners of the Irene Ryan Award for Acting, the highest honor for acting any college theatre student can receive. Rickaby was in the award-winning production of *Homesteaders*.

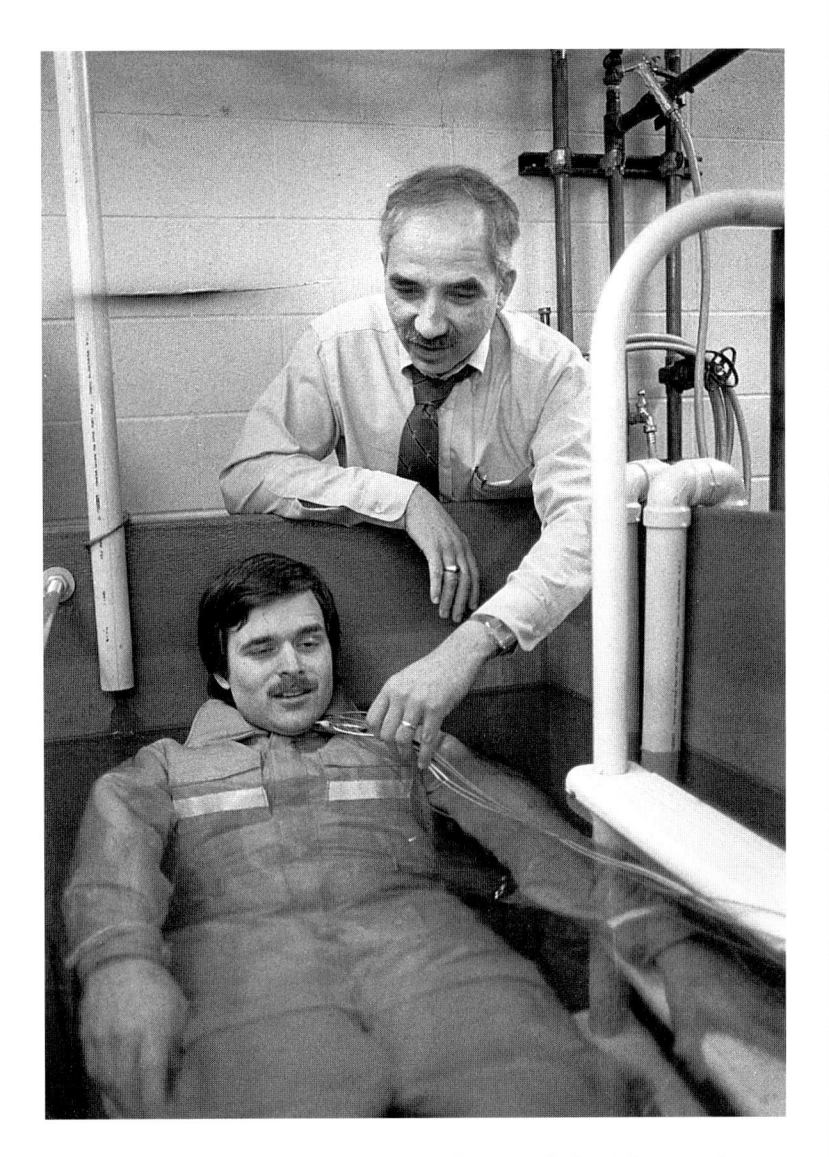

Robert Pozos and Larry Wittmers, professors of physiology at the UMD School of Medicine, began hypothermia research in the late 1970s. Above, Pozos adjusted the water temperature as medical student John Ibsen, '90, served as a test subject in 1988. Under Wittmers' direction, the research continues and has expanded to general aspects of temperature regulation in both hot and cold environments.

Richard Durst, professor of theatre, became dean of the School of Fine Arts in 1988. "In 1982, the theatre faculty decided that we were not satisfied with being just 'another arts program,' but wanted to be the best undergraduate theatre program in the Midwest," Durst said. "I watched, sometimes in awe, the strong commitment to training, both inside and outside the classroom. Classes were stimulating, and the production values unequaled. We had recruited a superb group of students. . . . And as the successes happened, students flocked to the program. Rehearsals were electric and the product was more than any of us dreamed.

"One of the proudest moments in my life was to read the words of a Washington critic who said that our production of *Homesteaders*, the first of the three shows we took to the American College Theatre Festival finals, was the 'finest of theatre available in our American colleges and universities!' Only one other program in this country has taken a production to the Kennedy Center more than twice."

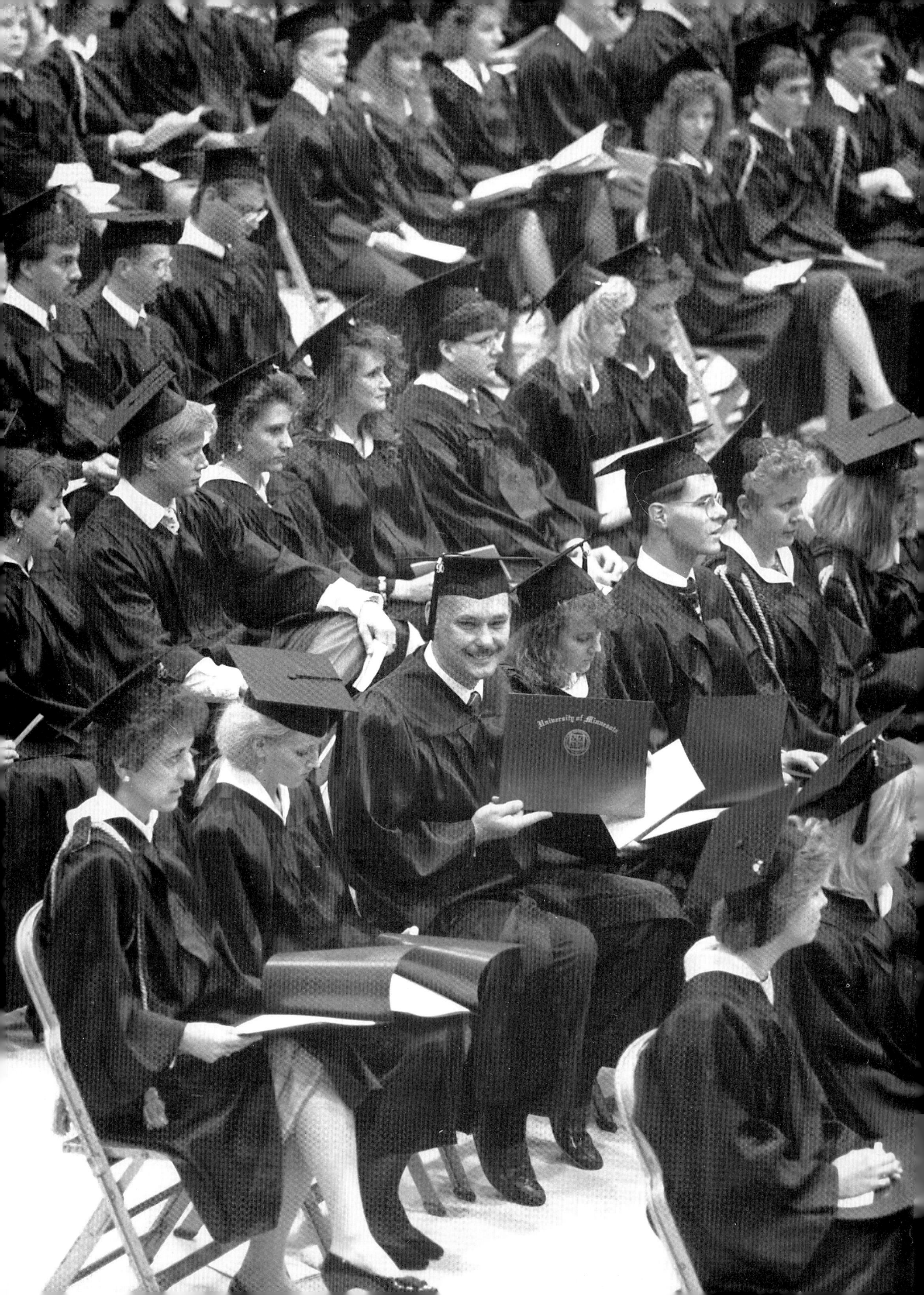
University of Minnesota

THE IANNI YEARS: A DECADE OF GROWTH

1987–1995

UMD has developed impressively since its inception a century ago. This development, in terms of its physical size, its enrollment, and the number of its degrees and programs, justifies our celebration theme, "UMD Comes of Age." With this impressive record of progress in place, UMD should look forward to what the next steps in its development should be. No doubt further growth in enrollment and in additional programs should be part of that development. I hope that the right reason for numerical growth will be recognized. Growth in the number of students will not be progress in and of itself. Those who think that bigger is better in universities are misguided.

On the other hand, an increase in the number of students means the expansion of a university's intellectual capital if the institution grows programmatically as well as numerically. When a university is wealthy in intellectual capital, it has truly matured. When its faculty encompass a wide variety of fields of learning, when these faculty include a number of innovative thinkers and a number of creative doers, and when those faculty stimulate students to move on to insightful and creative lives, then the university has developed into the kind of institution for increasing and disseminating knowledge and wisdom that has always been hoped for in Western society.

CHAPTER SIX
THE MATURE UNIVERSITY
By Lawrence Ianni

Left: Richard Jacobson, an industrial technology major, was one of several hundred students to receive their degrees at UMD's 1990 fall commencement ceremonies on November 18 in Romano Gymnasium. More than thirty-seven thousand students have graduated from UMD, DSTC, and the Duluth Normal School in the first one hundred years.

Lawrence Ianni served as chancellor of UMD from 1987 to 1995. He is seen here with his wife Mary Ellen.

An early Halloween guest greeted Lawrence Ianni and Mary Ellen Ianni at Ianni's inauguration ceremony on October 30, 1987.

The UMD gymnasium was renamed Romano Gymnasium on January 16, 1988, in memory of Ralph Romano, former UMD coach and athletic director. Chancellor Lawrence Ianni and Barbara Romano, Ralph's widow, unveiled this memorial plaque at the special dedication ceremony.

Left: UMD successfully completed its four-year capital campaign in 1988, raising $12,957,329 in gifts and grants for endowed faculty positions, scholarships, academic programs, and research. Martha B. Alworth tried out the chair her family received for establishing the Royal D. Alworth Jr. Professorship in Northern Circle Studies as Chancellor Ianni watched.

In 1989 a complex of three new residence buildings was named Goldfine Hall in honor of Duluth business leader Erwin L. Goldfine, who served twelve years as a regent of the University of Minnesota. Goldfine and his wife Beverly unveiled this sign at the special dedication ceremony. The Beverly and Erwin Goldfine Scholarship for Excellence was established in 1987. The scholarship rewards outstanding academic achievement.

Matti Kaups, right, professor of geography and ethnohistory, was knighted by the government of Finland on February 21, 1991. Kaups was decorated with the Knight First Class of the Order of the White Rose by Garth Castren, Finnish consul general, in recognition of his extensive research in and efforts to preserve Finnish culture.

The mature university is a center of learning where the faculty as well as the students are learning. With regard to these factors, it is appropriate for UMD to compare itself with its distinguished older sibling in the Twin Cities. That institution has reached full maturity through the achievements of its Walter Hellers, Norman Borlaugs, and Robert Penn Warrens and the students whom they schooled to go forward and make their own records of achievement. When several generations of such scholars and students follow one another, a university can truly be said to have matured. That maturity will provide its own evidence of its existence. One thinks of Ralph Waldo Emerson's Phi Beta Kappa lecture at Harvard in which he charged the students to remember that the great minds they have studied were themselves once merely young people working in libraries. Such perspective only comes with the self-confidence that one can build on the best that has been thought and created.

UMD has begun this last and most important stage of the process of maturation. It has a faculty rich in accomplishment and even richer in potential. It has students, who, if guided to realize their full potential, will match the best of their generation in their achievements. I have no doubt that UMD's second century will see the attainment of this most desirable yet rare level of maturity, and I have no doubt that the city of Duluth, which has always supported and cherished its university, will be even prouder of it than it is now.

Lawrence A. Ianni served as Chancellor of UMD from 1987 to 1995. He is now a professor of English at UMD.
Reprinted with permission from The Duluthian *(March-April 1995).*

UMD broke into the top fifteen ranking of regional universities in the October 15, 1990, issue of *U.S. News & World Report.* **That same year UMD also was ranked a "Best Buy" by** *Money* **magazine. UMD has received top rankings in four of the five years since.**

On September 21, 1991, UMD paid a lasting tribute to a handful of the Bulldog greats of yesteryear by inducting twelve individuals into its newly established Athletic Hall of Fame. Among those in the charter group were, from the left, hockey All-American Keith "Huffer" Christiansen, former Notre Dame and Green Bay Packer Head Coach Dan Devine, Lou Barle (the first Bulldog to play at the professional level in the NFL in the late 1930s), All-American and former Kansas City Chiefs running back Ted McKnight, basketball star Mike Patterson, and three-sport standout John Vucinovich. Other charter members included NHL performers Curt Giles, Tom Kurvers, and Glenn "Chico" Resch, the late and long-time athletic director and football and basketball coach Lloyd Peterson, seven-sport letter winner and former University of Minnesota volleyball coach Stephanie Schleuder, and the late Maurice Gorham, one of the early pioneers of Bulldog football, basketball, and track.

Pierce in March of 1992 by dedicating the Robert F. Pierce Speech-Language Hearing Clinic. Pierce came to UMD in 1951, serving in the Department of Speech for many years as well as developing a program in communication disorders. It was through Pierce's tireless efforts that UMD opened the original Speech-Language Hearing Clinic.

The 1992–93 *Statesman* staff gathered for a photograph.

UMD grabbed the college basketball spotlight in 1990–91 thanks to the heroics of two senior centers—Jay Guidinger and Dina Kangas. Guidinger, the first individual ever to be named the Northern Sun Intercollegiate Conference's Player of the Year on three occasions, closed out his Bulldog playing years as the school's all-time leader in points, rebounds, and blocked shots. In November 1991 he added another entry to his lists of firsts when he became the first Bulldog to play in the NBA with the Cleveland Cavaliers. Kangas left the UMD program as the proud owner of twenty-three club single-game, single-season, and career records. The three-time NAIA All-American also scored more points (an NCAA Division II-record 2,810) during her four seasons than anyone in the history of Minnesota collegiate basketball, men or women.

Facing page: In what became more or less an annual rite of spring, the Bulldog men's basketball team paid eight straight visits to the NAIA National Tournament between 1985–92 while the women's team qualified for seven berths in that same event from 1988 to 1994.

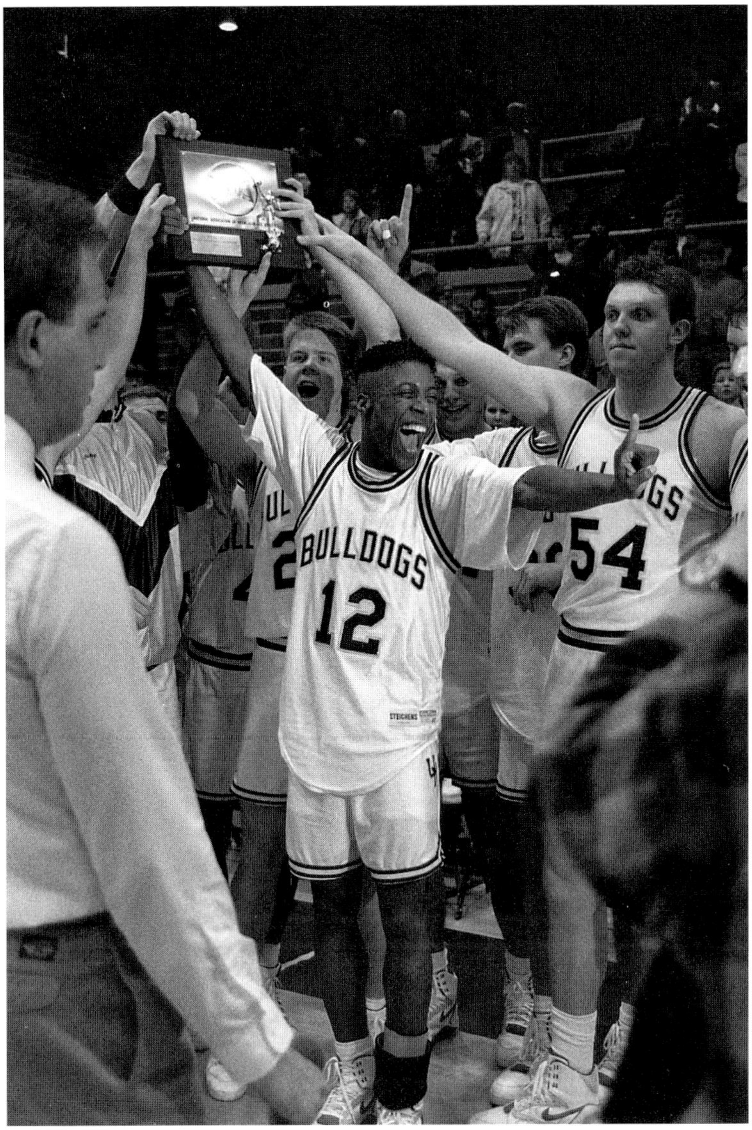
BULLDOGS
12
54

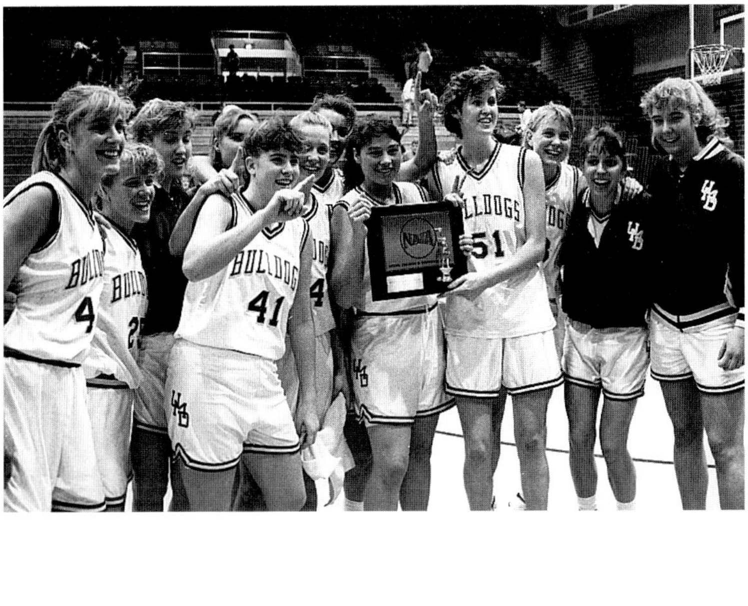
BULLDOGS
41
51

REMEMBERING OLD MAIN
by Klaus Jankofsky

Fog blanketed Old Main's arches when Vice Chancellor of Finance and Operations Greg Fox, at left, turned the Old Main property over to Duluth Mayor Gary Doty, a UMD graduate, on October 18, 1993. The property was donated to the City of Duluth Parks Department.

For almost twenty-five years now, we have lived within a block and a half of Old Main. The lower campus, and Old Main in particular, had impressed me as a landmark of particular interest from the first moment I had come to Duluth for a 1967 interview with Ray Darland, Bob Heller, and members of the English department who were seeking a suitable medievalist for the rapidly expanding English and liberal arts program. My wife Kay and I moved here in 1969 from Germany to make our home here and raise our children, and to find that Duluth was a place to satisfy our hopes for natural beauty, lifestyle, and personal and professional commitments.

For years we went for walks through the neighborhood. Often I played with my children at Old Main, making dandelion garlands in the spring or belly-crawling through the high grass around the big clump of bushes, pretending to be tigers and jungle beasts on the prowl, and sledding down from Washburn in the winter before the Holy Rosary hills became more challenging. I remember theatre performances at Old Main, among them an impressive *Glass Menagerie*, teaching some "Rusty Ladies" courses in what later came to be called Women's Seminars and then the University for Seniors, and one of Professor Harriet Viksna's famous "Ringeltanz" in the old gym with a huge multicolored parachute as a canopy over the dance floor.

We have been proud, in a strangely personal way, to show this part of the city and the lower campus to visiting friends and dignitaries from the U.S. or abroad, almost as a treasured possession. The very structures of Old Main and the spirits that inspired them, and the ghosts of the past (students, teachers, benefactors to UMD, and politicians and citizens working on behalf of UMD) still speak to that phase of our communal history. In this sense, the loss of Old Main is a heartfelt loss.

UMD's original home was merely a ghost of its former self on the morning of February 23, 1993, after a fire destroyed Old Main.

For me, a professor of Old English, Middle English, and European languages and literature, a study of the past is rich in sights and observations relevant to the present. In the Middle Ages, but even more so in the Renaissance, the ruins and antiquities of Carthage and Rome inspired poets, painters, architects, and philosophers who thought of themselves as thoroughly modern (and we, in retrospect, see them as such). Can we not, here in Duluth, achieve something similar, even on a modest scale, by preserving the ruin of Old Main as a ruin, as a monument to the city's and the state's hopes and aspirations for its future, as a dedication to the past that was nobly inspired, and as a record of the connection between destruction and death and the hope that gives life and renewal? As of this writing, the demolition is almost complete. Only the central and east and west arches are still standing. May they serve as dignified reminders and a landmark of our academic and civic past.

Klaus Jankofsky, professor of English, learned about the arson that had destroyed Old Main the morning after the fire. This essay is excerpted from a longer piece, "Old Main Is a Part of This Community's History," which he wrote for the March 11, 1993, issue of the UMD Statesman. *It is excerpted by permission.*

Above: This 1954 springtime photo suggests the timeless architectural appeal of Old Main, which UMD closed as a classroom facility in 1985.

Because the ruins of Old Main were considered a hazard to health and safety, UMD was forced to demolish the building. Now only the original Old Main arches remain to remind us of UMD's beginnings.

Daniel Schorr, veteran reporter-commentator, presented the Dalton LeMasurier Memorial Lecture on April 29, 1993. Schorr also was a special guest at the first UMD Alumni Association Recognition Evening held the same day.

The Ward Wells Field House was dedicated on October 1, 1993, in memory of the late Ward Wells, head of UMD's physical education department for many years and a strong UMD and community advocate for physical education as part of the liberal arts program. Wells' sons Tom and Jeff, left and right, attended the ceremony with their mother Ingrid.

Chancellor Ianni cheered while holding the ribbon at Duluth City Hall on March 14, 1994, at the end of Ken Foxworth's first 154-mile "Run for Excellence" from St. Paul to Duluth. Foxworth, who was the African American student advisor at UMD for four years, raised more than $100,000 on his two runs to benefit the Harry Oden Scholarship for minority and disabled students.

Harry Oden spoke in front of Duluth's City Hall to the crowd of supporters who welcomed Ken Foxworth home. A 1963 graduate of UMD, Oden was the speaker for the 1990 fall commencement ceremony and received the Distinguished Alumni Award for his work as an educator and his community activism. Oden has enthusiastically recruited students for UMD and served as the chairperson for the UMD 100-Year Celebration Committee. He is the president of the Milwaukee chapter of the Alumni Association.

David A. Vose, economics professor, served as dean of the School of Business and Economics from 1978 to 1992. He has since returned to the classroom. "Teaching is one of my greatest pleasures . . . seeing students leave UMD well-prepared for the future and with good feelings towards the institution," Vose said.

Reflecting national trends in higher education, non-traditional students have become an increasingly significant group in UMD's undergraduate and graduate programs.

Right: Members of the Twin Cities chapter of the UMD Alumni Association and friends enjoyed a picnic before the Minnesota Twins game on May 17, 1994, at the Metrodome in Minneapolis. At the picnic, chapter President Frank McCray, '67, presented certificates to UMD coaches in honor of their dedication to Bulldog athletics. The Twin Cities chapter, the first official geographic chapter of the Alumni Association, was formed in 1994.

Minnesota's two most successful college football coaches—UMD's Jim Malosky, left, and St. John's John Gagliardi, right—were guests of Minnesota Governor Arne Carlson as part of a special tribute honoring these two legends on May 25, 1994, at the Governor's Mansion in St. Paul. A gathering of about three hundred attended the event, which reunited a pair of individuals who have more than eighty years of head coaching experience between them. Malosky is the winningest coach in the history of NCAA Division II football while Gagliardi ranks second in career victories among all collegiate head coaches.

Students can make study spaces anywhere on campus.

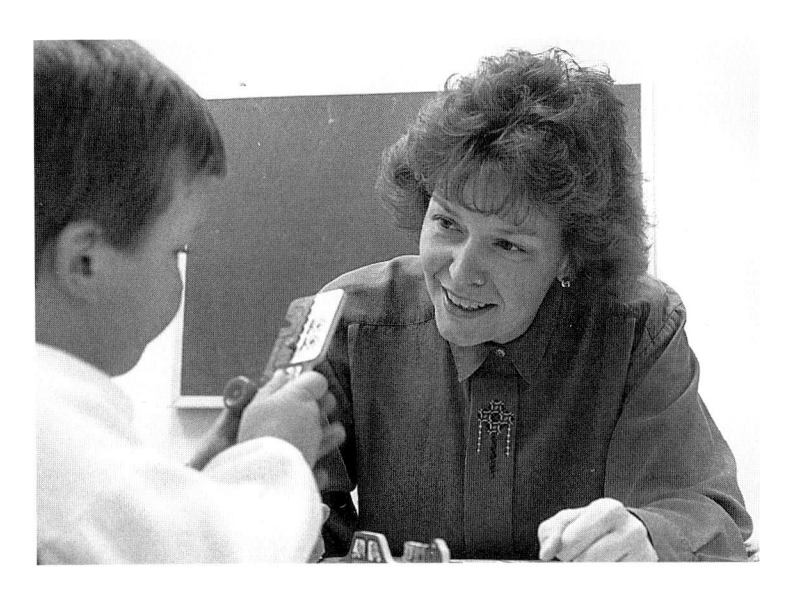

Carol Sazama, Scottish Rite Clinic coordinator, worked with a young client. The clinic helps hundreds of young children with language and hearing problems.

Professor Gerald A. Hill, left, director of the Center of American Indian and Minority Health, consulted with students.

Judge Gerald Heaney was a University of Minnesota regent from 1964 to 1965. Since 1966 he has served as the Eighth District Circuit Court of Appeals judge. "UMD is the most important public institution in northeastern Minnesota, just as the University of Minnesota is the most important public institution in the entire state," he said. "Not only do we train people for jobs in this region, but we provide economic, cultural, and social advantages that cannot be overestimated. The UMD faculty provides research and other assistance to the community. I think that probably the most important thing we have in terms of growth of the community in the future is to have a strong and active UMD."

Sabra Anderson, dean of the College of Science and Engineering, is one of a relatively small number of female deans heading engineering and science programs at U.S. universities. Anderson joined the UMD faculty as a professor of mathematics and statistics.

A student tried out her cross-country skis on the trails in the Bagley Nature Area.

Winter fun at UMD comes in many guises.

Above: Chancellor Ianni welcomed U.S. President Bill Clinton to UMD on November 4, 1994, thirty-one years after President John F. Kennedy's visit to campus.

Left: Those who did not get a chance to hear President Clinton speak in the Romano Gymnasium waited enthusiastically in Ordean Court as the president made his way through the crowds.

Cheng-Khee Chee was a UMD librarian from 1965 to 1994 and a professor of art from 1979 to 1994. His watercolor paintings for Douglas Wood's book *Old Turtle* won him world acclaim. "My ultimate goal in painting is to achieve Tao, the state of effortless creation, which is beyond craftsmanship and artistry," he said. "From my Chinese tradition, I was taught that 'teaching by action is more effective than teaching by words'—this is particularly important when it comes to teaching art. If you want to be an artist, you should be a scholar first—you must have a background in spirituality . . . you must have the compassion to understand, recognize and respect diversity . . . you must build a close bond between you and your students," Chee reflected.

Ruth A. Myers, former co-director of American Indian Programs in the School of Medicine, received an honorary doctorate at the 1994 fall commencement. The Ruth Myers Professorship in American Indian Education, one of the endowed chairs at UMD, honors her leadership.

Dance instruction is a significant part of the theatre program at UMD.

Karen Stromme, the women's basketball head coach since 1984, has coached her teams to six Northern Sun Intercollegiate Conference titles (NSIC), seven straight wins in the National Association of Intercollegiate Athletics (NAIA) District thirteen tournaments, and seven straight appearances in that league's national tournaments. She is also the chair of the USA Basketball Team Selection Committee, which picked the U.S. entry for the 1996 Olympic games. She was named the 1994–95 NSIC Coach of the Year. Dale Race, the men's basketball head coach since 1984, has been the winningest coach in the UMD basketball program with seven NSIC titles and eight appearances in the national tournaments. Race also has been selected NSIC Coach of the Year six times.

Students enjoyed a winter game of volleyball.

Top: Eve Cole, philosophy professor and associate dean of the College of Liberal Arts, writes a monthly ethics column for the *Duluth News-Tribune*.

Right: Hundreds of alumni, students, faculty, and friends celebrated UMD's one hundredth birthday during a special party on March 31, 1995, in the Marshall Performing Arts Center.

Happy 100th Birthday UMD 1895-1995

Downtown Duluth joined UMD's one hundredth birthday celebration with a banner strung across a Superior Street skywalk.

Right: Sunny days brought out soccer players.

Above and next page: The various campus musical groups continue to provide many opportunities for musicians.

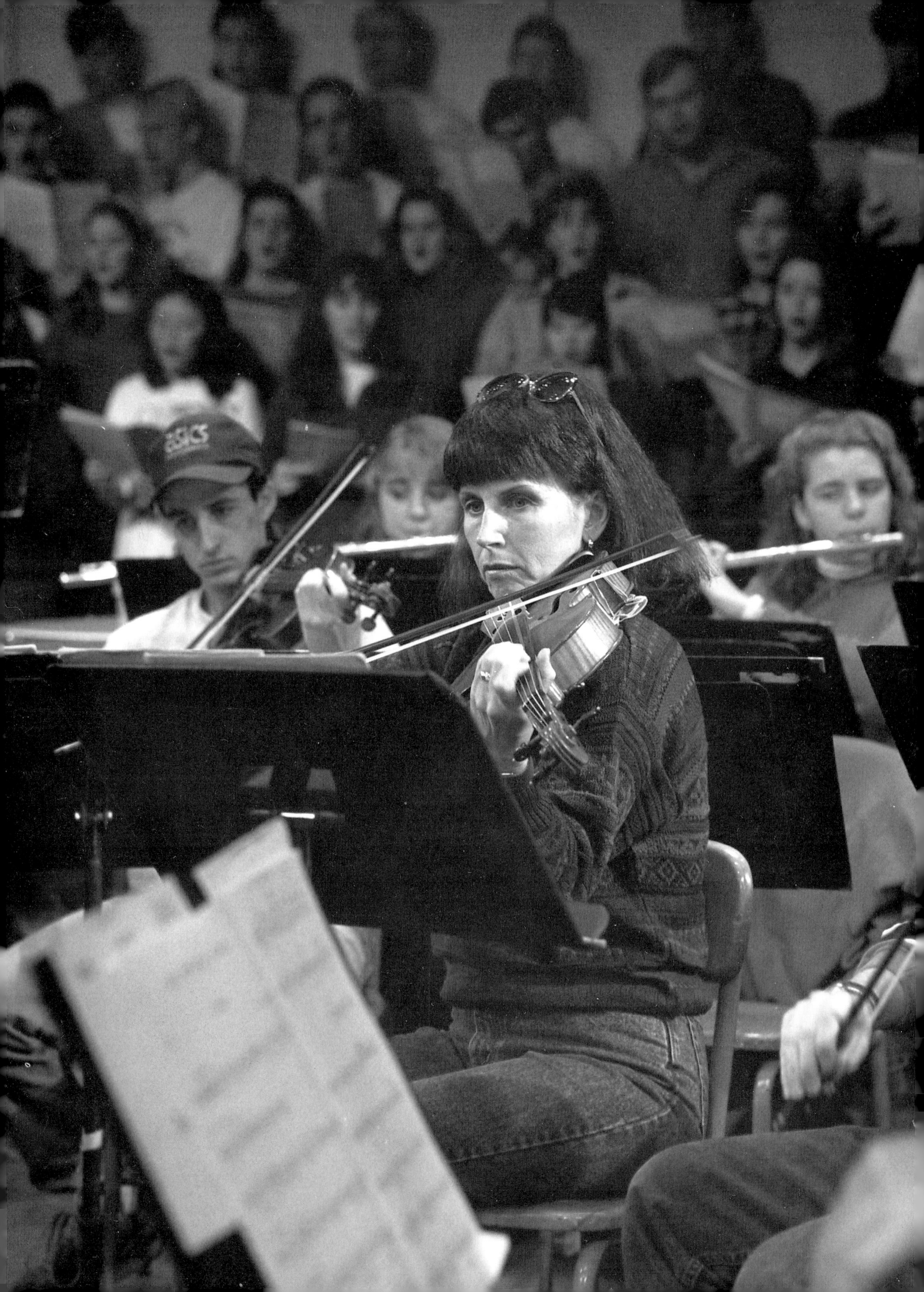

The UMD Alumni Association float brought the one-hundred-year celebration message to the Christmas City of the North Parade on November 17, 1995, in downtown Duluth. The float was designed by Robert C. Murray, who graduated from UMD in 1952 with a double major in business administration and economics. One of UMD's strongest alumni supporters, Murray received the Distinguished Service Award during the first UMD Alumni Association Awards program at the 1995 Homecoming activities. Murray's service to UMD includes designing the 1993 award-winning Alumni Association float, serving as president of the UMD Alumni Association and the Blueline Club, and founding UMD's first scholarship for student athletes.

Right: Computerized registration, financial statements, and transcript information has made the "business" of being a student much easier.

205

Budding horticulturists receive hands-on training in the Life Sciences greenhouse.

Facing page, top: The thirty-member UMD Alumni Association Board of Directors meets quarterly and serves as a liaison between UMD and the Alumni Association. Members of the 1995–96 board and guests who attended the fall 1995 meeting are, bottom row from the left, Chancellor Kathryn A. Martin, R. J. Falk, Bob Williams, Jack Ezell, Steve Bystedt, Janet Petersen, and Jim Shearer. Top row from the left are Associate Alumni Director Beth Brown, Kathy Roach, Julene Boe, Vice President Vicki Beaupre, Alumni Director Lucy Kragness, Bonnie Edwards, Cliff Sjolund, Thomas Hagen, Gary Waller, Diane Rauschenfels, Charlie Glazman, President Cindy Finch, University Relations and Development Director Diane Skomars, and Bruce Watkins.

The UMD Campus Center was dedicated during a special program on October 30, 1995. The new building provides classroom space and offices for the Department of Mathematics and Statistics, Achievement Center, Career Services, Admissions, and part of Continuing Education and Extension. Helping dedicate the building were, from left, former Chancellor Lawrence Ianni, Gerry Heller, widow of the late Chancellor Emeritus Robert Heller, Chancellor Kathryn A. Martin and Robert Carlson, chemistry professor and former vice chancellor for academic administration who chaired the building committee.

UMD Chancellor Kathryn A. Martin greeted and helped Sarah Moeller
and Peter Edstrom move into campus housing September 2, 1995.

CHRONOLOGY

by Doreen Hansen
and James Vileta

1895-1915

1895
April Duluth Normal School was authorized by an act of the Minnesota State Legislature. The City of Duluth was required to donate six acres of land for the campus.

1896
April Six acres of land at Twenty-third Avenue East and Fifth Street were donated by the City of Duluth and the Duluth Board of Education as a site for the new Normal School.

1897
The Minnesota State Legislature made an appropriation of $5,000 to build a foundation for the Normal School building.

1899
The Minnesota State Legislature appropriated $75,000 for erecting the "Main" building at the Duluth Normal School. Half of the funds were available in 1900, the rest in 1901.

1901
The February fire left only black walls of the original "Main" building structure. The heavily insured building was reconstructed.

1901
April Dr. Eugene W. Bohannon of the Mankato Normal School was selected as president of the Duluth Normal School at $2,500 per year.

1902
September Duluth Normal School started registration and oper-ations.

1903
June Seven women received the first diplomas granted by the Duluth State Normal School.

1906
September Washburn Hall, a "ladies dormitory," was completed and opened. Its cost was $35,000.

1909
A west wing costing $60,000 was added to the Main Building.

1910
September Torrance Hall opened as a dormitory.

1915
An east wing was added to the Main Building, and construction of the auditorium began.

1916-1929

1916
The Duluth Normal School raised its admission standards by requiring a high school diploma.

1921
April Duluth Normal School received a new name. An act of the Minnesota State Legislature redesignated state normal schools as State Teachers Colleges. Accordingly, Duluth Normal School thereafter became known as Duluth State Teachers College (DSTC). The law also authorized the State Teachers College Board to grant appropriate degrees to persons who completed a prescribed four-year curriculum of studies in these institutions.

1923
September A four-year curriculum leading to the Bachelor of Education degree was offered for the first time.

1927
May The new laboratory school and heating plant were dedicated.

1927
June The first bachelor degrees were awarded at DSTC.

1929
May The State Teachers College Board, meeting in St. Paul, established a four-year course at DSTC. The new course qualified students for every kind of public school work.

1929-1937

1929
December The DSTC basketball team played its first scheduled game. The team lost 38-23 to Duluth Junior College.

1929
October Less than forty men were enrolled in DSTC in 1929. By 1931, more than two hundred men were enrolled. Men remained a minority, about 20 percent, from 1931 to 1937.

1930
September DSTC played its first football game against Northland College.

1930
October Male students protested discrimination in class officer elections.

1931
January First ever DSTC hockey game was played against Duluth Central High School. Central won 3-0.

1933
School athletes chose the bulldog as the school's mascot.

1937
A. I. Jedlicka wrote a bill that would require the Regents of the University of Minnesota to establish a branch in the city of Duluth.

1937
March University of Minnesota President Lotus D. Coffman issued a document opposing branches of the University in Minnesota.

1937
May Dr. E. W. Bohannon, sixty-eight, announced his plan to retire on January 1.

1946
March Warren Stewart of St. Cloud, president of the State Teachers College Board, heard complaints against the administration of DSTC President Herbert Sorenson. Some faculty claimed that conditions had

1947
July The name and organization of the college were changed to University of Minnesota, Duluth Branch (UMD). UMD was established as a branch college of the University of Minnesota with permission to grant the Associate in Arts, Bachelor of Arts, and Bachelor of Science degrees. Raymond C. Gibson, DSTC president, would be retained as head of UMD with the title "Provost."

1948
August An Air Force ROTC unit was authorized for the UMD campus.

1949
April Provost Gibson announced that, beginning with the 1949 summer session, graduate level courses would be offered at UMD.

1950
June Provost Gibson announced his resignation, effective June 30, to join the education division of the Inter-American Affairs Institute as chief administrator in Lima, Peru.

1953
June Provost King announced his resignation to accepted the presidency of Kansas State Teachers College at Emporia, effective in September.

1953
July A sixteen-acre tract of wooded land adjoining the UMD campus was given to the Board of Regents by Dr. and Mrs. William R. Bagley and their daughter Dr. Elizabeth C. Bagley. With this donation, UMD had a 196-acre campus. This gift, along with the Rock Hill gift of 1951, was dedicated as the Bagley Nature Area in 1974.

1953
September Dr. Raymond W. Darland, academic dean and acting provost, was named UMD's third provost.

1953
September UMD received a gift of $400,000 from Stephen R. Kirby toward the building of a student center.

1937-1941

1937
August Dr. Herbert F. Sorenson, professor of education at the University of Minnesota, was named to succeed Bohannon who announced his retirement effective January 1, 1938. Sorenson was president from 1938 to 1946.

1940
May The last "May Fete" ceremony was held at DSTC.

1941
Olcott Hall, Twenty-third Avenue East and First Street, was formally accepted by DSTC. It was presented by Mrs. Leonard Elsmith of New York (nee Dorothy Olcott) and her sister, Mrs. Elizabeth Olcott Ford of LaJolla, California, daughters of J. W. Olcott, a former president of the Oliver Iron Mining Company. The home was remodeled for use as a music conservatory. Mr. and Mrs. George P. Tweed purchased and presented the spacious Joseph B. Cotton home to DSTC. Cotton, general solicitor for the Oliver Iron Mining Company, built the mansion in 1916 at a cost of $200,000.

1946-1947

deteriorated since 1944. Later, "In an atmosphere charged with tension and tears," Dr. Herbert F. Sorenson announced his resignation at a special assembly. Dr. E. H. Pieper was immediately named acting president by Arthur M. Clure, the DSTC resident director.

1946
May Thirty-six-year-old Dr. Raymond C. Gibson, director of teachers' training at Central State Teachers College, Stevens Point, Wisconsin, was elected president of DSTC, effective July 1.

1946
August The Minnesota State Teachers College Board approved DSTC becoming a four-year liberal arts college, beginning in the fall of 1946.

1947
February The city planning commission reserved a vacant 160-acre diamond-shaped property west of Woodland Avenue near the Chester Park school as a possible site for the proposed University of Minnesota branch. This property became known as the "Nortondale Tract."

1947
February The Minnesota House began consideration of a bill by Representative A. B. Anderson for the conversion of the DSTC into a branch of the University of Minnesota.

1947-1951

1951
June Acting Provost John E. King, who had served in this capacity since June 1950, was appointed provost at the University Regents meeting in St. Paul on June 1, 1951.

1951
June UMD received two large residences from Mr. and Mrs. Royal D. Alworth Sr. The properties were located at 2605 and 2617 East Seventh Street and were adjacent to the George P. Tweed mansion (site of the first Tweed Gallery) given to UMD in 1950.

1951
July Groundbreaking ceremonies for the Health and Physical Education Building were held. The building was occupied September 14, 1953, and was dedicated on December 12, 1953. The building was renamed Romano Gymnasium in honor of Ralph A. Romano on January 16, 1988. Total project cost: $1,602,000.

1951
November Northeastern Minnesota civic leaders viewed "UMD–1970," a scale model of the new UMD campus plan, at Duluth's Kitchi Gammi Club. This plan, formed under the leadership of Provost King, provided the campus with the blueprint it followed for the next two decades.

1953-1956

1953
October Master of Arts degrees were offered through the Graduate School at UMD.

1954
April Groundbreaking ceremonies were held for the UMD Library. Dedication ceremonies were held February 24, 1956, with an address by Vice President Malcolm Willey.

1954
September Groundbreaking ceremonies for the Kirby Student Center, with Stephen R. Kirby turning the first spade of earth, were held. Kirby opened on June 21, 1956.

1954
November Construction of Vermilion Hall began. Units were occupied in the fall of 1956.

1956
May Groundbreaking ceremonies were held for the Humanities Building and Tweed Gallery. The new Tweed Gallery, within the Humanities Building, was dedicated in 1958. Construction began for the Mathematics-Geology Building (renamed Heller Hall on September 30, 1988). The building was completed in the spring of 1965.

1956-1960

1956
September UMD joined the National Collegiate Athletic Association (NCAA).

1956
November A campus radio station began broadcasting at 940 on the AM dial from the basement of Washburn Hall with a quarter watt of power. Call letters KUMD were officially assigned in April 1958.

1958
April Groundbreaking ceremonies were held for the Social Science Building (renamed Cina Hall on May 4, 1985, for former University Regent Fred Cina).

1958
May Construction for Burntside Hall began. A public open house was held a year later.

1958
May Olcott Hall, former home of UMD's Music department since 1939, was sold.

1958
October Tweed Gallery was officially named and dedicated.

1959
June The Board of Regents unanimously voted to change the name of the Duluth campus from University of Minnesota, Duluth Branch, to the University of Minnesota Duluth.

1960
September Construction began for the Education Building (renamed Bohannon Hall on May 22, 1974 to honor Eugene W. Bohannon, first president of Duluth Normal School and Duluth State Teachers College). The dedication was held on April 11, 1962. The project was completed in the summer of 1966.

1960
October Mrs. Alice Tweed Tuohy was the first woman honored with the University of Minnesota Regents Award.

1960-1966

1960
November Construction began for the Industrial Education Building (renamed Voss-Kovach Hall on October 9, 1982). The building opened for classes in February, 1962, and an official dedication was held on April 5, 1963.

1961
February Eric Sevareid, CBS news, gave the first Dalton A. LeMasurier Memorial lecture. The lecture series honored the memory of Duluthian Dalton LeMasurier, founder of KDAL-TV.

1962
November University Regent Richard L. Griggs announced that he would retire from his position after serving for twenty-four years.

1963
September President John F. Kennedy addressed delegates to the Northern Great Lakes Region Conference on Land and People in the UMD Physical Education Building.

1964
October The newly completed UMD Campus Club was dedicated.

1965
October Construction of the Marshall W. Alworth Planetarium began. Marshall W. Alworth provided funds for the building. It was completed in the spring of 1967 and dedicated in June of 1967.

1965
November The bronze statue of French explorer Daniel Greysolon, Sieur du Lhut, created by sculptor Jacques Lipchitz, was unveiled in conjunction with the dedication of a major addition to Tweed gallery.

1966
August Groundbreaking ceremonies for Griggs Stadium were held. The stadium was named to honor Regent Griggs.

1966
September Groundbreaking ceremonies for the Life Science Building were held. The building was occupied in 1968.

1968-1971

1968
September UMD announced that it would sponsor the University Artist Series, a concert series featuring outstanding national and international musicians.

1968
October Groundbreaking ceremonies were held for the Classroom-Office Building (renamed A. B. Anderson Hall at a dedication to prominent Duluth legislator A. B. Anderson on September 8, 1973). The building was occupied in the fall of 1970.

1969
June Groundbreaking ceremonies were held for Lake Superior Hall. It was completed during the summer of 1971.

1969
December Groundbreaking ceremonies were held for the Administration Building (renamed Darland Administration Building on March 12, 1982, to honor Provost Emeritus Raymond W. Darland). The building was occupied in the summer of 1971.

1970
April Plans for apartment-style housing using prebuilt modular units (the original Village Apartments) were announced by UMD and University officials. Completion was set for the fall quarter.

1971
July Groundbreaking ceremonies were held for the Residence Hall Dining Center. The center was occupied in July 1974.

1971
August The Air Force ROTC program announced it would begin enrolling women in the fall of 1971.

1971
September Groundbreaking ceremonies were held for Marshall Performing Arts Center. The dedication was held on February 3, 1974.

1971
November A plan to develop UMD into a major "University Center" was explained to newsmen by Provost Darland and Vice Provost for Academic Administration David Vose. The plan envisioned development of a School of Business, School of Fine Arts, Lake Superior Basin Studies Program, and Interdisciplinary Studies Program.

1972-1977

1972
June Groundbreaking began for Stadium Apartments.

1972
July Groundbreaking began for the Classroom-Laboratory Building (renamed Marshall W. Alworth Hall). The building was completed in the summer of 1974.

1972
September The first class of twenty-four students at UMD School of Medicine began it's program.

1973
July Groundbreaking began for the Physical Education Field House. The building was occupied on March 10, 1975.

1974
October The Board of Regents approved UMD academic reorganization from four divisions to two colleges and four schools: College of Letters and Science, College of Education, School of Business and Economics, School of Medicine, School of Fine Arts, and School of Social Work.

1976
February Provost Darland announced his resignation as of June 30, 1976 after twenty-eight years at UMD, twenty-three of them as provost.

1976
June Groundbreaking ceremonies were held for the Medical School. The building was occupied February 19, 1979, and a dedication ceremony was held on September 15.

1976
October Groundbreaking ceremonies were held for the Health Science Library. The building was occupied in the fall of 1977.

1977
January Robert L. Heller was named provost at UMD to succeed Raymond W. Darland. Heller had been acting provost since 1976.

1977
November University President C. Peter Magrath opened the Court Gallery at Tweed Museum of Art.

1977-1979

1977
November The University of Minnesota Sea Grant Program officially was established by the National Oceanic and Atmospheric Administration.

1978
April Construction began for Junction Avenue Apartments (renamed Cuyuna Hall and Mesabi Hall on March 12, 1982).

1978
October Provost Robert L. Heller announced the establishment of the Thea Johnson Lecture Series featuring national and international speakers. Johnson was a Duluth businesswoman and strong supporter of UMD.

1979
January The combined estates of Jonathan, Simon, and Milton Sax were bequeathed to the Tweed Musuem of Art. A one million dollar gift for the purchase of original artworks came from the Milton Sax estate. Paintings, sculpture, and other artworks were to be purchased from the interest of the "Simon, Milton, and Jonathan Sax Purchase Fund." In 1987 the Sax gift funded construction of the Sax Gallery, a sculpture conservatory.

1979
May The Northern Bible Society of Duluth presented UMD with one of the largest Bible collections in the U.S.

1979
July Glensheen, the thirty-nine-room Congdon mansion, was opened to public tours for the first time. In the first five days, thirty-eight hundred persons toured the mansion and grounds.

1979
October Groundbreaking ceremonies were held for the School of Business and Economics Building. The building was occupied in the fall of 1981 and the dedication was held on March 7, 1982.

1980

1980-1986

September The first Study-in-England group of students left for a year at the University of Birmingham in England.

1980
October The Duluth chapter of the Minnesota Education Association (UMDEA) became the first faculty bargaining unit in a runoff election with AAUP.

1980
November Groundbreaking ceremonies were held for Oakland Avenue Apartments (individually named Oak, Aspen, Birch, and Basswood Halls).

1983
July The Natural Resources Research Institute was created by Governor Rudy Perpich, Minnesota legislators, and community leaders.

1984
March UMD's hockey Bulldogs won the WCHA title by defeating North Dakota 12–6.

1984
May UMD's Library was designated as a Federal Depository Library by the U.S. Government Printing Office.

1984
September Establishment of the annual Albert Tezla Scholar/Teacher Award was announced by Donald K. Harriss, vice provost for academic administration.

1986
June Chancellor Heller announced his retirement from the University, effective June 30, 1987.

1986
July NRRI reached an agreement with the U.S. Steel mineral research laboratory at Coleraine. The agreement included the sale of laboratory and research equipment at the Coleraine facility and the lease of portions of land, several buildings, and some mobile equipment.

1986
December The new Engineering Building opened.

1987-1994

1987
May UMD's theatre production *Homesteaders* was judged best in the region and was selected by the American College Theatre Festival to play at the Kennedy Center in Washington, D.C. A second production, *Blue Collar Blues*, also won both awards in 1989 and a third production, *Standing on My Knees*, won both awards again in 1991.

1987
July Lawrence A. Ianni took office as chancellor at UMD. Ianni formerly was provost and vice president for academic affairs at San Francisco State University.

1989
June A complex of three new UMD residence halls was named Goldfine Hall at a dedication ceremony honoring Erwin L. Goldfine, who served twelve years on the Board of Regents before retiring in 1987.

1990
October UMD was rated as the ninth best regional university in the Midwest in a survey by *U.S. News and World Report* magazine. UMD consistently has earned high ratings ever since.

1993
February Old Main, UMD's original building on the lower campus built at the turn of the century, was destroyed in an arson fire the night of February 22. The site later was donated to the City of Duluth for a park.

1993
May UMD School of Medicine was selected for a special recognition achievement award by the American Academy of Family Physicians.

1994
May Chancellor Ianni announced he would step down after serving as UMD's chancellor since 1987.

1994
September A new Library Building task force was appointed. The task force established seeks support to erect a new library building.

1994-1995

1994
November U.S. President Bill Clinton appeared at a political rally at UMD.

1995
March UMD's School of Medicine appeared in the March 20 issue of *U.S. News and World Report*'s "America's Best Graduate Schools." UMD was tied for second place out of 125 in the nation for rural medicine. Sixty percent of School of Medicine graduates now practice in communities of fewer than fifty thousand.

1995
March A one-hundred-year birthday celebration for UMD was held in MPAC.

1995
September George "Rip" Rapp, professor of geoarchaeometry and the director of the Archaeometry Lab at UMD, was named a Regents' Professor of the University of Minnesota, the first from a campus outside of the Twin Cities, and one of only twenty system-wide.

1995
October The new UMD Campus Center was dedicated in "The Wedge." A separate dedication for the Campus Center sculptures, "Untitled," commissioned from Minneapolis sculptor Steven Woodward, was held in the Campus Center plaza.

1995
November Kathryn A. Martin, formerly dean of the College of Fine and Applied Arts at the University of Illinois at Urbana, Champaign, was inaugurated as eighth chancellor of the University of Minnesota Duluth. She is the first woman chancellor in the University system.

UMD REFLECTIONS II

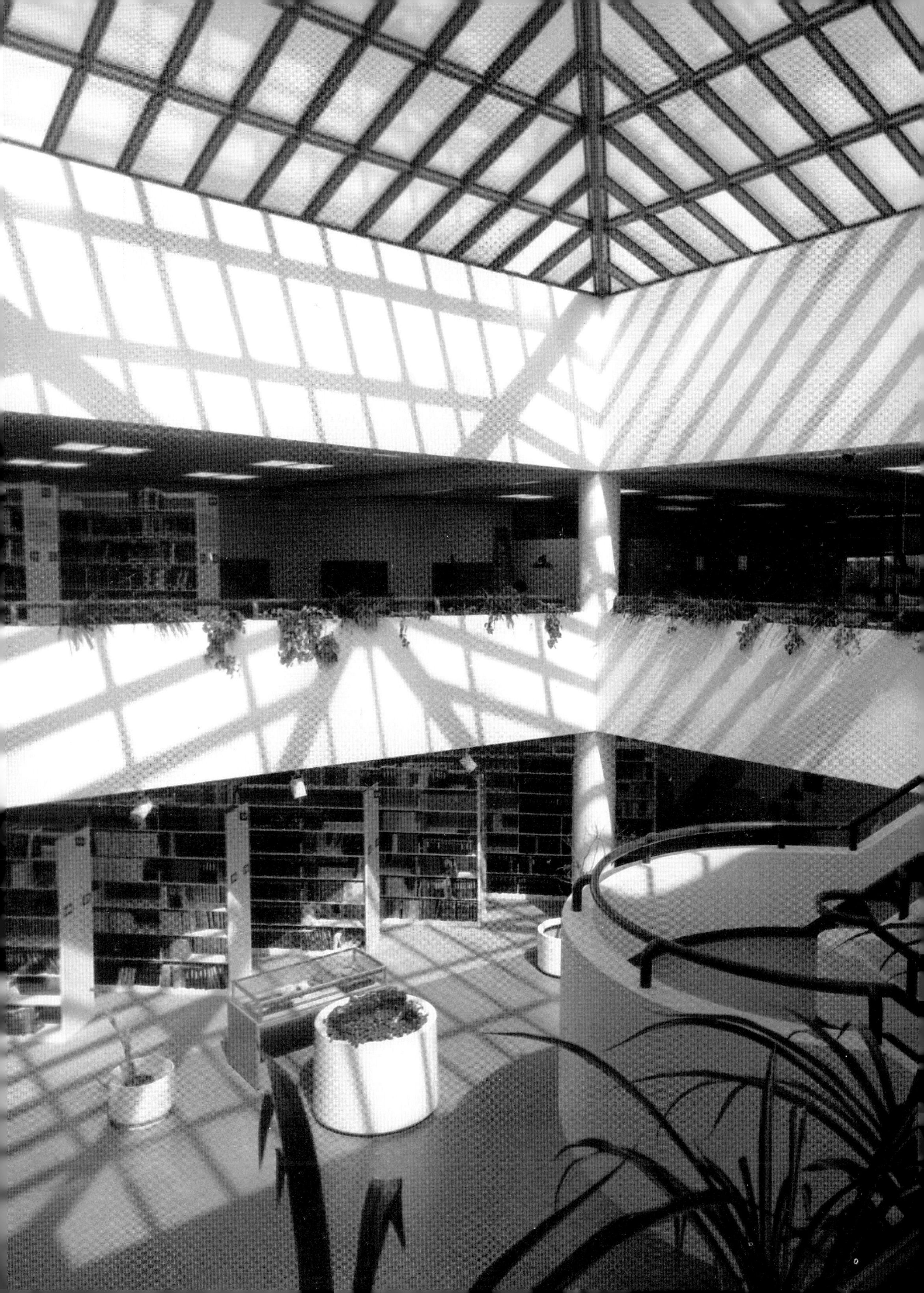

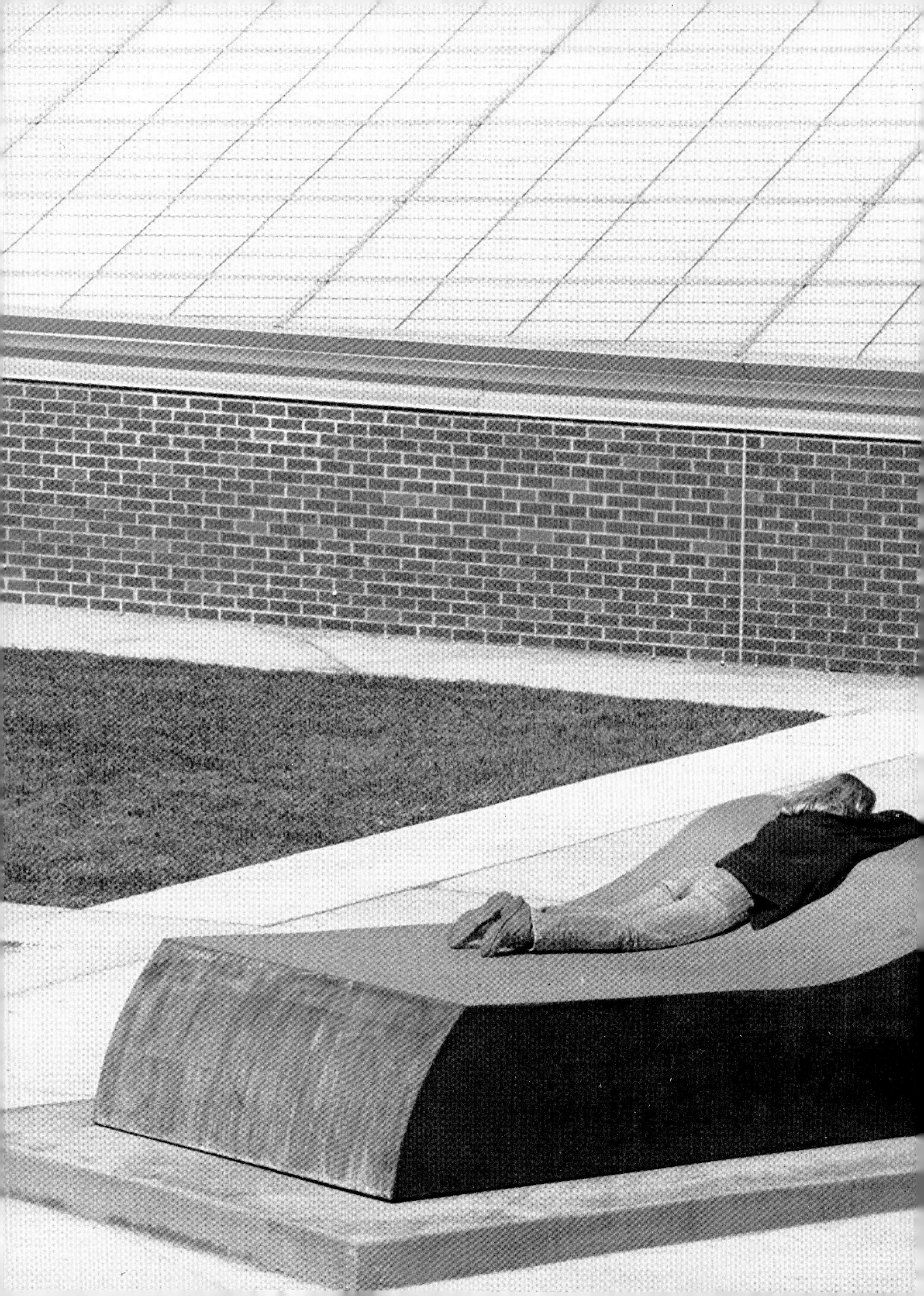

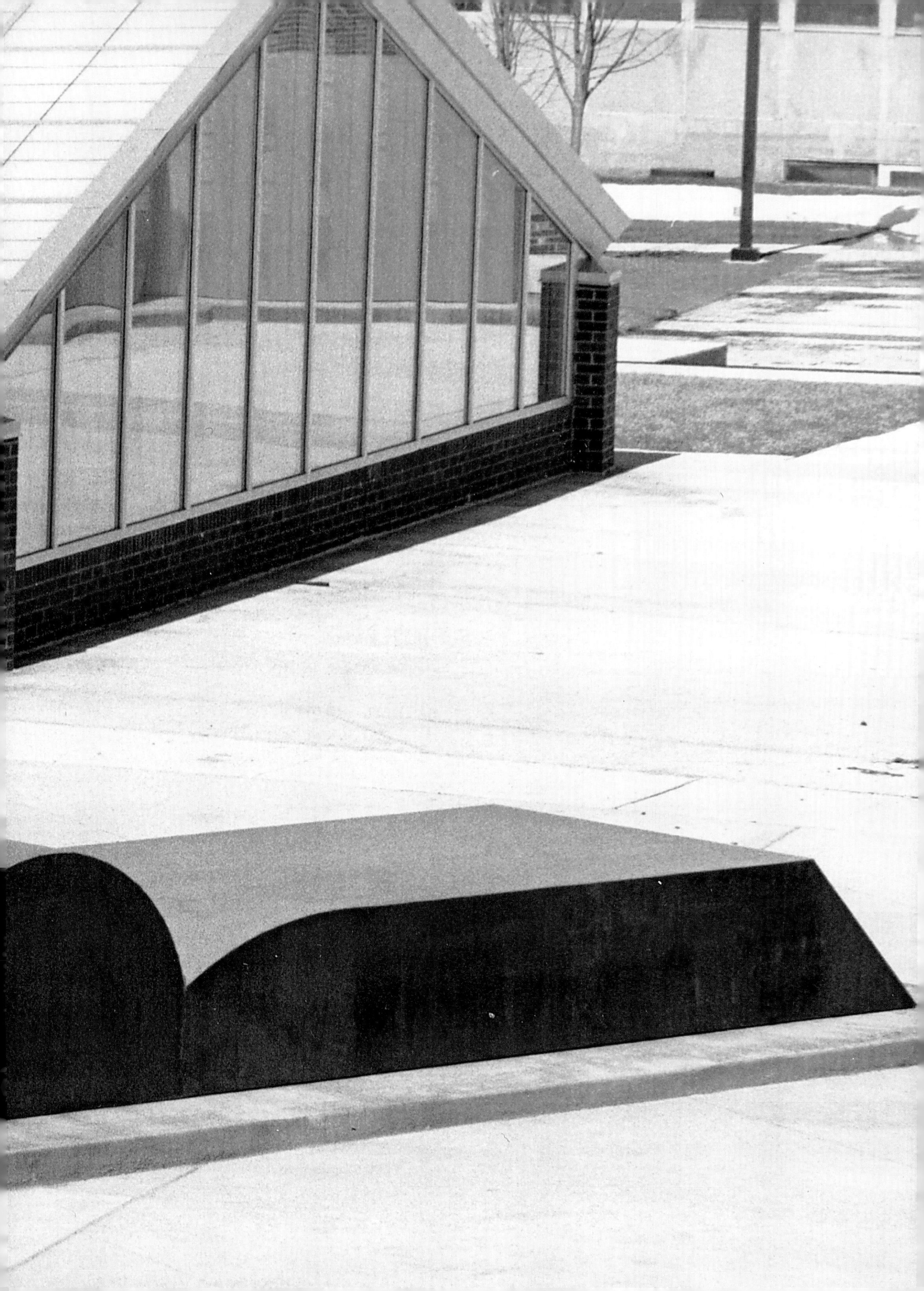

216

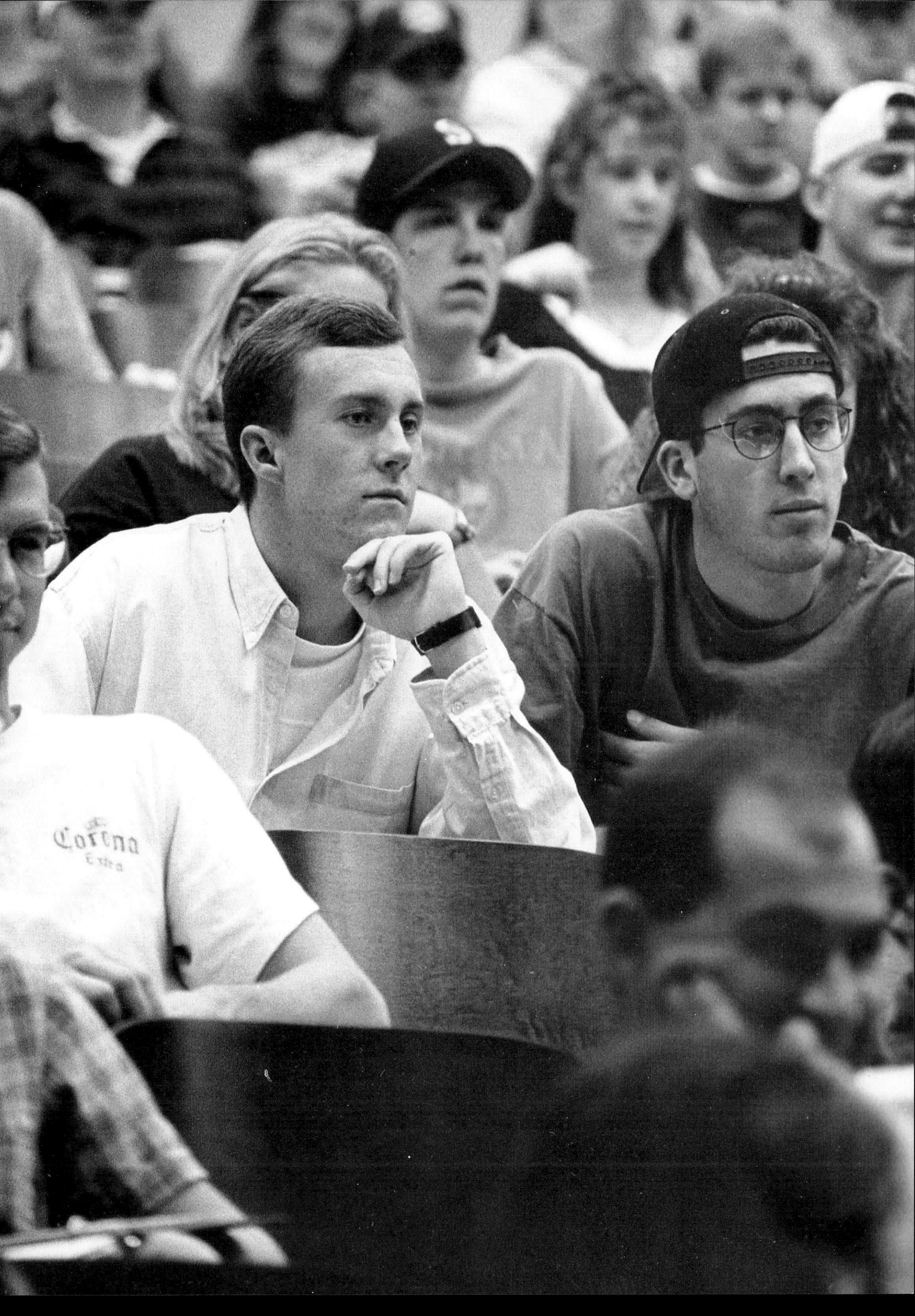
Corona
Extra

INDEX

A
A. B. Anderson Hall, 41
Achievement Center, 206
Admissions, 206
African American, 191
Ahlen, A. H., 32
Alamisa, Betsy, 146
Alpha Nu Omega, 113
Alumni Association Recognition Evening, 190
Alumni Association, 129, 190, 191, 205, 206
Alworth mansion, 103
Alworth Planetarium, 105, 111
Alworth, Marshall W., 111
Alworth, Martha B., 181
Alworth, Royd D. Jr., 164, 181
American Association of University Professors (AAUP), 168-170
American College Theatre Festival, 173, 177
American Indian communities, 165
American Indian culture, 136
American Indian Learning Resource Center, 91
American Indian Programs, 169, 195, 198
American Indian Studies, 88, 91, 127
Anderson, A. B., 30, 35, 39, 41, 42
Anderson, Ann, 165
Anderson, Clarence, 146
Anderson, Sabra, 196
Angel Flight, 124
Anishinabe Days, 136
Annette, Dr. Kathy, 129
Anthony, Ray, 73
Antigone, 18, 22
Archaeometry Laboratory, 150
Athletic Hall of Fame, 51, 184
Auden, W. H., 94

B
Bacig, Thomas, 169, 170
Bagley Nature Area, 66, 143, 196
Bagley, Charles, 80
Bagley, Elizabeth C., Dr., 66, 143
Bagley, William R., Dr., 32, 66, 143
Bagley, William R., Mrs., 66, 143
Baker, Dale, 144
Baleziak, Louis, 43
Banning, Margaret Culkin, 16, 21, 38
Barle, Lou, 184
baseball, 104
basketball, 25, 104, 138, 186, 187, 199
Beaupre, Vicki, 206
Belthuis, Lyda C., 50
Berman, Mike, 94
Beta Phi Kappa, 60, 93, 95
Biology, Department of, 50, 57
Blatnik, John, 86
Board of Regents, 38, 54-55, 82, 105, 115, 164, 165, 173
Bobbitt, Betsy, 10
Boe, Julene, 206
Bohannon Hall, 93
Bohannon, President Eugene W., 13, 14, 15, 16, 17, 18, 29, 30, 76, 93
Bohlke, Dale, 128
Boman, Thomas, 170
Borlaugs, Norman, 183
Bowers, Barbara, 128
Bowers, Betty, 128
Bowmann, Bessie Emily, 16
Bowyer, Helen Emily, 16
Boyce, William, 158
Boyer, Samuel H., Dr., 80, 81
Bridges, Robert W., 41, 93, 121

Brown, Beth, 206
Brown, Cyrus, 80
Brown, Gerald, 129
Buck, Fred W., 38
Buckhorns, 60
Burntside Hall, 148
Business Administration, Department of, 55
Business and Economics, School of, 142, 192
Bystedt, Steve, 206

C
Campus Center, 78, 135, 206
Campus Club, 104
Cap and Gown Day, 164
Caple, Ron, 131
Career Services, 206
Carlson, Arne, Governor, 193
Carlson, Richard, 44
Carlson, Robert, 206
Carnegie Commission on Higher Education, 84
Casey, Maria, 132
Center of American Indian and Minority Health, 195
Chamberlin, Thomas W., 50, 53, 93, 113
Charity Ball of 1952, 72
Chee, Cheng-Khee, 198
Cheerleaders, 37, 49
Chemistry Building, 59
Christensen, Anders, 108
Christensen, Chris, 108
Christensen, Donnan, 108
Christensen, Dory, 108
Christensen, Kenner, 108
Christensen, Odin, 108
Christiansen, Keith "Huffer," 112, 184
Christie, Virginia, 48
Cina, Fred A., 86, 115
Cinderella, 157
Clifford, Michael, 128
Clinton, William, President, 197
Close, Winston A., 66
Clure, Arthur M., 32, 38
Clure, Thomas, 112
Coffman, Phillip, 158
Cohen, Lee, 128
Cole, Eve, 200
College of Education and Human Service Professions, 164
College of Letters and Science, 91, 150, 161
College of Science and Engineering, 49-50, 150, 196
College Playdays, 40
Collins, Hollie, 127
Commencement, 17, 131, 179
Commission on Women, 163
Communist Party of America, 92
Conant, Jonathan, 150
Continuing Education and Extension, 206
Corson, Jim, 32
Cothran, John C., 50
Cotton, Joseph, 32, 37
Coultrap-McQuin, Susan, 165
Council of Religious Advisors, 152
Crassweller, Frank, 32
Crawford, Dean, 169
cross-country, 104
Culkin, Mabel, 16, 21

D
Dahl, Clarence, 41, 42
Dalton LeMasurier Memorial Lecture, 81, 116, 190

Darland Administration Building, 110, 121
Darland, Provost Raymond W., 18, 50, 66, 71, 75, 76, 77, 78, 80, 81, 89, 90, 91, 93, 94, 98, 102, 104, 109, 110, 111, 113, 114, 115, 118, 121, 131, 146, 158, 188
Darling Observatory, 81
Darling, Jack, 81
Date, Mary, 114
Davidson, Emmett, 85
DeLisle, Joe, 171
Denney, Jim, 161
Deteret, David, 128
Devine, Dan, 51, 184
Devine, JoAnne, 51
Dickerman, Charles K., 66
Dickerman, Gilbert G., 66
Dickson, Macy, 146
Distinguished Alumni Award, 191
Dorsey, Tommy, 103
Doty, Gary, 188
Doty, Ralph, 86
Douglas, William O., 94
Downs, Allen, 62
Dr. Faustus, 61
du Lhut, Daniel Greysolon, Sieur, 80, 100-101, 105, 140
Dudley Experimental Theatre, 130
Dudley, Marjorie Congdon, 130
Duluth Advisory Committee, 55
Duluth Business Index, 162
Duluth Normal School, 13, 14, 15, 16, 22, 23, 24, 25
Duluth State Teachers College, 13, 15, 16, 19, 22, 25, 26, 27, 29, 30, 31, 32, 33, 34, 36, 37, 38, 39, 40, 41, 42, 43, 45, 47, 49, 50, 56, 57, 176. 179
Duluth, 66, 161, 188, 202
Duluth-Superior Symphony Orchestra, 165
Dunn, Roy, 42
Durst, Richard, 177

E
Earth Days, 126, 127
Edstrom, Peter, 207
Education Building, 93
Education, Department of, 59
Edwin Eddy Professorship in Neurocommunication Disorders, 164
Ehlers, Henry J., 50
Ehlers, Mary Ann, 62
Ehlert, Jackson K., 49
Elefson, Amanda, 16
Elgart, Les, 96-97
Elizabethan Dinners, 129
Ellington, Duke, 103
Ellis, Sue, 146
Elwell, Mary I, 33, 50
Emerson, Ralph Waldo, 183
Engagement Ball, 113
Engineering, 160, 161
enrollment, male, 25, 26, 34
Erickson, Chad, 138
Ezell, Jack, 206

F
Falk, Dennis, 165
Falk, Robert, 10, 44, 206
Fall Freshman Dance, 36
Fathers, John, 149, 150
Fayle, Professor, 103
Feast of Nations, the, 153
Fedo, John, Mayor, 161
Ferraro, Geraldine, 170

field hockey, 104
Finch, Cindy, 206
Fine Arts, Department of, 49
Fine Arts, School of, 158, 177
Finland, 182
Fischer, Roger, 169
Football, 25, 26, 27, 36, 104, 152, 193
Fox, Greg, 121, 188
Foxworth, Ken, 191
France, Alfred, 86
Freshman Camp, 166, 167
Friedman, Thomas, 151

G
G.I. Bill, 34
Gagliardi, John, 193
Gamma Theta Phi, 85
Geology, 145, 154, 175
Gibson, Provost Raymond C., 30, 39, 41, 44, 45, 47, 49, 50, 51, 53, 54, 55, 56, 57, 59, 66, 88
Giles, Curt, 184
Giliuson, Virginia, 28
Glass Menagerie, 188
Glazman, Charlie, 206
Glensheen, 105, 136
Glick, James, 69
Glick, Wendell P., 90, 150, 169
Goldfine Hall, 182
Goldfine, Beverly, 182
Goldfine, Erwin L., Regent, 81, 86, 146, 161, 162
Goldish, Robert, 81
golf, 104
Goode, Bruce, 150
Gorham Maurice, 184
Graduate programs, 80, 137
Grandchamp, John, 37
Grant, Christabel, 149
Grant, Dorothy, 32
Grant, James, 149
Grant, James, 149, 150
Grau, Craig, 169
Graybeal, Elizabeth, 50, 71
Great Depression, 25, 34, 63
Green, Sue, 37
Greysolon, Daniel, 80, 100-101, 105, 140
Griggs Field and Stadium, 104, 112
Griggs Hall, 148
Griggs, Regent Richard L., 18, 38, 41, 50, 71, 76, 77, 89, 91, 94, 1105, 115
Gronseth, Glenn, 162
Gruba, Gene, 73
Guidinger, Jay, 138, 186
Gustafson, Earl, 86
Gustafson, Richard, 128
Guys and Dolls, 92

H
Hable, Rose, 48, 59
Hall, Gus, 91, 92
Hall, Patty, 151
Hansen, Doreen L., 9
Harrington, John, 161
Harrington, Vern, 80
Harry Oden Scholarship, 191
Hawk Ridge, 59
Hayes, Harold, 61, 68
Health and Physical Education, Department of, 50
Health Science Library, 156
Heaney, Gerald W., Judge, 86, 151, 154, 161, 195
Hedman, Stephen, 10
Heffernan, Colleen, 151

219

Helleloid, Burton, 128
Heller Hall, 173, 174
Heller, Chancellor Robert L., 50, 80, 81, 102, 121, 145, 146, 149, 150, 151, 154, 161, 164, 165, 168, 171, 172, 173, 174, 188, 206
Heller, Gerry, 173, 206
Heller, Walter, 183
Hello, Dolly, 130
Hendrickson, A. Dean, 169
Higgins, Ray, 86
Hill, Gerald A., 195
Himango, George F., 88
Hirschbock, Frank J., Dr., 30
History, Department of, 16
Hobey Baker Memorial Award, 163
Hockey, 104, 112, 138, 149, 163, 167, 171, 184
Hoffman, Eleanor, 169
Hofslund, Jack, 59
Hols, Edith J., 165
Holt, Aonas Rebecca, 16
Home Economics Building, 159
home economics, 23, 102, 159
Home Economics, Department of, 32, 103
Home Management House, 103
Homecoming parade, 49
Homecoming, 25, 28, 41, 49, 48, 51, 59, 60, 94, 95, 96-97, 109, 114
Homesteaders, 151, 173, 176, 177
Hoover, Roy, 150
Horne, Olive, 16
Houle, James, 114
House, Mary Sue, 128
Hubert, John, 128
Humanities Building, 77
Humanities, Department of, 37, 77
Humphrey, Hubert H., Vice President, 86, 111
Hylden, Eric, 146

I
Ianni, Chancellor Lawrence A., 10, 179, 180, 181, 183, 191, 197, 206
Ianni, Mary Ellen, 180
Ibsen, John, 177
Importance of Being Earnest, The, 61
International Club, 153
International Wheelchair Olympic Games, 174
Irene Ryan Award for Acting, 176

J
Jack Rowe Chair in Electrical and Computer Engineering (Minnesota Power), 173, 174
Jackson, Donald, 81
Jacobson, Richard, 178, 179
Jacott, William, 81
James, George, Dr., 84
Jankofsky, Klaus, 10, 150, 188-189
Jedlicka, A. I., 32
Jerina, Jeris, 93
Johns, Allan, 128
Johnson, Jim, 171
Johnson, Joann, 117
Johnson, John F., 161
Johnson, Lyndon B., President, 98, 127
Johnson, Myrna, 92
Johnson, Viena, 30
Jones, S. F., 19
Jordan, Harvey, 151
Joseph and the Amazing Technicolor Dreamcoat, 135

Josephs, Adrienne, 158
Junior Prom, 73

K
Kane, Maureen, 128
Kangas, Dina, 138, 186
Karnis, Mike, 32
Katz, Virginia, 128
Kauppi, Sharon, 109
Kaups, Matti, 182
KDAL-TV, 81
Kennedy, President John F., 79, 94, 127, 177, 197
King, Mrs. John, 59
King, Provost John E., 46, 50, 53, 55, 59, 63, 66, 71, 75, 88, 102
Kirby Lectures and Convocations Committee, 128
Kirby Student Center, 77, 89, 104, 106-107, 172
Kirby, Stephen R., Mrs., 89
Kirby, Steven R., 77, 89
Kitchi Gammi Club, 129
Kovach, Frank, 33
Kragness, Lucy, 10, 206
Kulick, Marsha Bevard, 174
Kunstler, William, 128
Kurvers, Tom, 184

L
La Brosse, Francis (Frenchy), 154
Laboratory School, 16, 21, 86, 102
LaDue, Edward Sr., 128
Lakela, Olga, 35, 49
Lalich, Michael, 154, 155
Languages and Literature, Department of, 49
LaRoque, Arleen, 85
LaRoque, Dennis, 85
Latham, Jane, 28, 37
Leadbelly, 54
Lease, M. Harry, 150
Leestamper, Bob, 72
Lehman, Betty, 37
Leiviska, Shirley, 62
Leslie, Pattie, 146
Levy, Esther, 16
Library, 21, 86, 156, 160, 162
Lichty, Richard, 170
Life Sciences Building, 139, 206
Lindquist, Maude L., 47
Lindquist, Maude, 33
Lipchitz, Jacques, 80, 105
Liscomb, Charles F., 38
Lloyd Hawley Band, 34
Lucas, Steve, 128
Luukkonen, Lloyd, 28
Lyon, Harold A., 32

M
M Club, 63
MacTaggart, Bette, 131
Maddy, Jane E., 163, 165
Magnuson, Toni, 128
Magrath, C. Peter, 154, 161
Malosky, James S. "Mo," 91, 193
Mankowski, Patricia, 131
manual arts, 23
Marchetti, Robert J., 161
Margaret Mitchell Curator of the Tweed Museum, 164
Marinucci, Chris, 163
Marriage Ball, the, 103
Marsden, Ralph W., 154
Marshall Performing Arts Center, 105, 130, 139, 140, 200

Marshall W. Alworth Planetarium, 81, 105, 111
Marshall, Caroline, 130
Marshall, Julia, 130
Marshall, Willena Marie, 16
Martin, Chancellor Kathryn A., 7-8, 10, 132, 206, 207
Martin, Fletcher, 82, 83, 93
Martini, Edward A., 32
mascot, 22, 27
Master of Liberal Studies, 150
Mathematics and Statistics, Department of, 206
Mathematics-Geology Building, 173, 174
Matsch, Charles, 160
Maus, Patricia, 9
May Fete, 12, 18, 50
McCray, Frank, 10, 108, 192
McDonald, Mike, 144
McGee, Tim, 151
McGintey, Mary, 146
McGuckin, Eugene, 81
McIntyre, Jim, 36
McKnight, Ted, 152, 184
Medicine, School of, 19, 80, 82, 84, 86, 88, 128, 138, 164, 169, 173, 177, 198
Mendenhall, A. A., Mrs., 32
Menotti, Gian Carlo, 168
Merritt, Elizabeth, 16
Meyer, Cecil, 162
Meyer, Howard, 150
Michoy, Nancy, 146
Miller, Glenn, 103
Miller, John, 146
Miller, R. Dale, 33, 49
Minnesota Education Association, 168
Minnesota Intercollegiate Athletic Conference, 98
Minnesota Power, 161, 174
Minnesota Repertory Theatre, 155
Minnesota Sea Grant Extension Program, 144
Minnesota State Legislature, 13, 17, 19, 38, 39, 41-42, 82, 84, 86
Minnesota State Teachers College Board, 30
Moeller, Sarah, 207
Mondale, Walter, Vice President, 170
Money, 183
Montague Hall, 159
Montague, William K., 115, 159
Moore, Warren S., 41, 42, 81, 86
Moos, Malcolm, 78, 115
Moran, Jackie, 9, 96-97
Moran, Ken, 9-10
Morrill, James L., 34-35, 38, 69, 89
Morse, Mary, 10
Morse, Wayne, 98
Moscow State University, 171
Movilla housing, 124, 133
Mullin, Mary, 117
Murdock, Donald, 169
Murray, Bob, 48, 112, 205
Music, Department of, 33, 49, 60, 165
Music, Jerry, 92
Myers, Ruth A., 164, 198
Myles, Gerald A., 32

N
Nash, Ogden, 73
National Association of Intercollegiate Athletics (NAIA), 186, 199
National Education Association, 168
Native Americans into Medicine, 169
Natural Resources Research Institute, 19, 154, 155

NCAA Division II football, 193
NCAA Division II-basketball, 186
Nelson, Dionne, 160
Nelson, Glenn, 158
Nelson, James, 169
Nelson, Janet, 62
Ness, John, 116
North Vietnam, 129
Northeastern Minnesota Historical Center, 9, 150
Northern Intercollegiate Conference, 104
Northern Minnesota Council for Medical Education, 81, 86
Northern Sun Intercollegiate Conference, 186, 199
Northland College, 27
Nortondale Tract, 39, 50, 57, 68, 75
NRRI's Coleraine Minerals Research Laboratory, 175
Nye, James G., 35, 38, 39
Nygaard, Bob, 10
Nyquist, Deb, 132
Nysteun, Sally, 151

O
O'Reilly, James, 128
Oberstar, James, 86
Oden, Harry, 10, 191
Odlaug, Theron O., 50, 57, 80
Ojakangas, Beatrice, 10, 102-103, 154
Ojakangas, Richard, 103, 154, 160
Olcott Hall, 56, 102
Old Main, 13, 17, 18, 19, 24, 57, 60, 63, 64, 65, 66, 82, 102, 176, 188-189
Old Turtle, 198
Olga Lakela Herbarium, 49-50
Olson, Karen, 113
Olson, Rodney, 128
Olympic games, 161, 199
one 100-Year Celebration Committee, 191
Onsgard, Kay, 69
Opheim, Vernon, 129
Ordean Court, 80, 101-102, 105, 140, 155, 197
Ordean, Albert O., 80, 140
Orvik, Bennett, 128
Owens, Bob, 86, 108
Owens, Mary Jane, 108

P
Pallansch, Michael, 135
Palmer, Ruth, 103
Paquette, Jerry, 10
Parker, Ruth, 72
Patterson, Mike, 184
Paulucci, Jeno, 86
Pavelich, Mark, 161
Pearce, Don, 160
Pearling, Lois, 32
Pearson, Betty, 28
Pederson, Denise R., 167
Perpich, Rudy, Governor, 154, 161
Petersen, Janet, 206
Peterson, Jerrold, 155, 162
Peterson, Lloyd W., "Pete," 27, 71, 121, 184
Petey Drive, 120
Phi Beta Kappa, 183
Phillips, Eunice, 149
Physical Education Building, 59, 68, 71, 79, 82, 98, 102
Pieper, Ezra H., 30, 47
Pierce, Robert F., 53, 184
Plumb, Valworth R., 50, 149

Plumb, Valworth, 93
Pogorelskin, Alexis, 10
Political Science, Department of, 32, 47
Post, Katherine, 16
Powless, Robert E., 91, 127
Pozos, Robert, 177
Prevost, Pat, 84
Psychology, Department of, 163
Puumala, Reinno, 81

R
Raab, Raymond, 150
Race, Dale, 199
Rajender Consent Decree, 170
Rajender, Shyamala, 170
Ramseyer-Northern Bible Society Museum Collection, 160
Rantala, Helen, 41
Rapp, Evelyn, 84
Rapp, George "Rip," 150, 161
Rapp, Keith, 128
Rauschenfels, Diane, 206
Reagan, Ronald, 170
Reasoner, Harry, 116
Regents of the University of Minnesota, 41, 94, 159, 173, 195
Regents' Professor, 150
Renslen, Sue Ann, 146
Resch, Glenn "Chico," 184
Research Laboratory Building, 19
Reserve Officers Training Corps (ROTC), 62, 124, 125, 131
Rickaby, Brett, 151, 176
Rickert, Lou, 71
Roach, Kathy, 206
Roach, Richard, 128
Robert F. Pierce Speech-Language Hearing Clinic, 184
Robert L. Heller Professorship in Geology, 164
Robin Hood, 25
Rock Hill, 66
Rock Pond, 143
Rockwell, George Lincoln, 90, 91, 92
Rogers, Carl, 94, 98
Rogers, Renae, 150
Romano Gymnasium, 98, 181, 197
Romano, Barbara, 181
Romano, Ralph, 98, 173, 181
ROTC, 41, 124, 125, 131
Roufs, Timothy G., Professor, 88
Rowe, Jack F., 161, 174
Royal D. Alworth Jr. Institute for International Studies, 150, 151
Royal D. Alworth Jr. Professorship in Northern Circle Studies, 164, 181
Ruikka, Margaret, 84
Ruth Meyers Professorship in American Indian Education, 164, 198
Rutherford, Bruce, 10
Ryan, Mary, 38
Rynda, Eleanor, 117

S
S.O.S. Week, 118
Saltus, Charles N., 16, 49
Sax Sculpture Conservatory, 158, 173
Sax, Jonathan, 158
Sax, Laverne, 158
Sax, Milton, 158
Sax, Simon, 158
Sazama, Carol, 195
Schegolev, Andrei, 131
Schengold, Nina, 151
Schlesinger, Arthur Jr., 94
Schleuder, Stephanie, 184

Schorr, Daniel, 190
Schroeder, George, Father, 152
Schultz, Roger, 130
Science and Mathematics, Department of, 49
Science and Physical Education, 66
Science Building, 50, 57, 82, 102
Scottish Rite Clinic, 195
Seligman, Felix, Mrs., 32
Sertich, Mike, 149, 163, 173
Sevareid, Eric, 81
Shearer, James, 159, 206
Sielaff, Richard O., 50, 55
Sigma Psi Gamma, 98
Sjolund, Cliff, 206
Skidmore, Connie Jo, 113
skiing, 104
Skinner, B. F., 94, 98
Skomars, Diane, 10, 206
Slack, Kay, 174
Smith, Arthur E., Professor Emeritus, 50, 93
Smith, David M., Professor, 88
Smith, Jarvis, 180
Smith, Phil, 61
Smith, W. C., Mrs., 32
Snow Ball, The, 103
Snow Week, 93
Social Development, School of, 164
softball, 104
Sorenson, 30, 31, 41, 54
Sorenson, Herbert, President, 29, 30, 57
Spencer, Jessica Marshall, 130
Spring Prom, 39
St. Louis County Board of Commissioners, 62
St. Louis County Historical Society, 9
St. Louis County Medical Society, 81
Stadium Apartments, 148
Stassen, Harold E., Governor, 46
State Normal Board, 20
State Teachers Board, 29
State Teachers College Board, 19, 30, 35, 54, 55
Statesman, 66, 73, 104, 185, 188
Stelzer, Gary, 128
Storch, Neil, 10
Strewler, Gordon, 80
Stromme, Karen, 199
Strong, Marjorie, 16
Student Association, 87, 91, 167
students with disabilities, 159, 174
study abroad program, 146
Study Abroad, 150
Study in England Program, 150
summer commencement, 146
Swanson, Jean, 150
Sweetheart of the Corps, 62
swimming, 104

T
Tamminen, Armas W., 93, 98
Taylor, Alyce, 37
Taylor, Herb, 61
Technology Development, 164
tennis, 104
Teppen, Roy, 112
Territorial Act of February 25, 1851, 35
Tezla, Albert, 63, 150
Thomas Theatre, John, 81, 135, 151, 157, 176
Thomason, Betty, 44
Thygeson, Walter, 27
Torrance Hall, 20, 38, 63, 88, 91, 102, 125
Torrance, Eli, 20
Toynbee, Arnold, 94

track, 25, 104
Triplett, Fred, 93
Trolander, Judith A., 165
Tropin, Uri, 171
Tsai, Bilin P., 165
Tuohy, Alice Tweed, 32, 37, 56, 57, 77, 80, 93, 137
Tuohy, Edward L., Dr., 94
Tweed Annex, 102
Tweed Gallery, 77, 80, 82, 93, 121
Tweed Hall, 32, 56
Tweed Museum of Art, 93, 104, 121, 137, 158
Tweed, George P., 32, 37, 56, 77

U
U.S. News & World Report, 183
Udall, Stewart, 127
UMD Alumni Association, 112, 114, 192, 205, 206, 207
UMD *Alumnotes*, 114
UMD Education Association (UMDEA), 168, 169, 170
UMD Fund, 174
UMD Library, 86
UMD Theatre, 135, 151, 157, 176
UMD's one hundredth birthday, 7-8, 179-180, 202
UMDEA, 169, 170
University Education Association (UEA), 169, 170, 170
University of Minnesota Regents Award, 94
University of Minnesota system, 69, 113, 155
University of Minnesota, 29, 30, 31, 32, 34, 35, 54, 55, 96-97, 169, 171, 172
University of Minnesota, Duluth Branch,43, 96-97
University of Minnesota, Minneapolis campus, 55
Urquhart, Helen, 16

V
van Appledorn, Ruth E., 50
Verrill, John E., 50
Vesterstein, Paul "Count," 68
Victoria Regina, 43
Vietnam War, 88, 96-97, 98, 121
Viksna, Harriet, Professor, 188
Vileta, James J., 9
Village Apartments, 124, 133, 148
Visiting Professorship in Finance and Management, 164
volleyball, 104
von Glahn, Gerhard E., 32, 47
Vose, David A., 192
Vucinovich, John, 184

W
Waage, Roger, 128
Wainstock, Sybil, 59
Waller, Gary, 206
Wallin, Dick, 48
Ward Wells Field House, 190
Warrens, Robert Penn, 183
Washburn Hall, 17, 42, 63, 71, 82, 86, 87, 102
Washburn, J. L., 16, 17, 18, 76
Watkins, Bruce, 206
Watson, Bill, 163
WCHA, 104
Weber, Max, 18, 22, 93
Weber, Ron, 59
Weinberg, Elliot, 66
Wells, Ingrid, 190
Wells, Jeff, 190
Wells, Tom, 190
Wells, Ward, 50, 190
Western Collegiate Hockey Association (WCHA), 98, 149
Westmoreland, H. E., 81
Wheat, David, 129
Whipps, Brian, 160
Wigg, Eleanor, 28, 38
Willcuts, Virginia, 16
Willey, Malcolm M., 34, 35, 56, 72
William R. Bagley Nature Area, 66, 143, 196
Williams, Bob, 206
Willman, Allen, 51
Wilson, John, 128
Wilson, Kim, 130
Wittmers, Larry, 177
Witzig, Frederick T., 82, 91
Wolff, Julius F., Sr., 32
Women's Athletic Association, 40
Women's sports, 104, 117, 138, 186, 199
Women's Studies, 163, 165
Women's Studies, Department of, 163, 165
Wood, Chester W., 50
Wood, Douglas, 198
World War II, 31, 32, 34, 59, 63, 66, 75
wrestling, 104

Y
Ylinen, Dona, 84
Youngdahl, Luther, Governor, 42, 43

Z
Zimmerman, Mary, 165

About the Authors

Neil Storch, professor of American history at UMD, joined the faculty in 1969. In addition to several recent articles and lectures on UMD history, he specializes in Upper Midwest regional and church history. He co-edited five volumes of *Upper Midwest History*, an interdisciplinary annual, and was one of four co-authors of *A History of the Duluth Diocese: Our Diocesan Century*. His scholarly articles and reviews also have appeared in *The Chronicle of Higher Education*, *Church History*, and *The Journal of Higher Education*, among others. He received his Ph.D. in history from the University of Wisconsin-Madison.

Ken Moran, a UMD graduate, has been UMD's campus photographer since 1958. He has taught UMD Continuing Education and Extension classes in basic photography in Mexico, England, and China. His photographs have been published in North America, Europe, Asia, Australia, and South America. Major exhibitions of his work have been presented at UMD as well as in Germany and China.